"HEED THE VOICE THAT MEOWS FROM WITHIN." —Lao Tzu Paws

As the kitties among us quest for what lies beyond their nine lives, a new feline, or a "catus novus," has begun to emerge, following such pathways to enlightenment as—

The Purrdictions of Nostracatus
The astonishing visions of the brilliant French Tabby who saw centuries into the future

The Care and Cleaning of Your Aura
A step-by-step guide to aura fluffing and last licks

Feline Future-Telling
The secrets of Pawmistry and other divination techniques revealed

Mind over Fur
A guide for using mind power to overcome catnip addiction, excessive appetite, fur balls, over-grooming, and other personal cat-astrophes

And Much More!

STEFANIE SAMEK is known as the "Cat Lady of Madison Avenue" for her work on the Whiskas and Sheba advertising campaigns. She is the author of A Cat's Christmas (Dutton) and Purring in the Light: NearDeath Experiences of Cats (Plume). She lives in Croton-on-Hudson, New York, with her husband and five cats. She can be reached at stefmeow@aol.com.

A CAT'S GUIDE
TO THE
MILLENNIUM

Spiritual Paths for the Enlightened Cat

Stefanie Samek

Illustrations by Larry Ross

A PLUME BOOK

PLUME
Published by the Penguin Group
Penguin Putnam Inc., 375 Hudson Street,
New York, New York 10014, U.S.A.
Penguin Books Ltd, 27 Wrights Lane, London W8 5TZ, England
Penguin Books Australia Ltd, Ringwood, Victoria, Australia
Penguin Books Canada Ltd, 10 Alcorn Avenue, Toronto, Ontario, Canada M4V 3B2
Penguin Books (N.Z.) Ltd, 182–190 Wairau Road, Auckland 10, New Zealand

Penguin Books Ltd, Registered Offices: Harmondsworth, Middlesex, England

First published by Plume, an imprint of Dutton Signet,
a member of Penguin Putnam Inc.

First Printing, October, 1997
10 9 8 7 6 5 4 3 2

 REGISTERED TRADEMARK—MARCA REGISTRADA

LIBRARY OF CONGRESS CATALOGING-IN-PUBLICATION DATA:
Samek, Stefanie.
    A cat's guide to the millennium : spiritual paths for the enlightened cat / Stefanie
Samek ; illustrations by Larry Ross.
        p.   cm.
    ISBN 0-452-27842-2
    1. Cats—Humor.   2. Millennium—Humor.   I. Title.
PN6231.C23S354   1997
818'.5402—dc21   97-11823
                                                                            CIP

Printed in the United States of America
Set in Goudy
Designed by Eve L. Kirch

BOOKS ARE AVAILABLE AT QUANTITY DISCOUNTS WHEN USED TO PROMOTE PRODUCTS OR
SERVICES. FOR INFORMATION PLEASE WRITE TO PREMIUM MARKETING DIVISION, PENGUIN
PUTNAM INC., 375 HUDSON STREET, NEW YORK, NEW YORK 10014.

To Richard C. Waldburger,
with whom it is an honor to share my life.

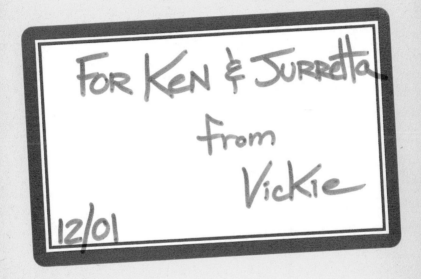

FoR KeN & JuRRetta
from
Vickie
12/01

ACKNOWLEDGMENTS

Thanks to Brugh Joy, David Lewine, Elizabeth Racine, Maria Napoli, Barbara Sarbin, Philip Kunz, Ana Maria Lozano, and my feline spiritual advisors, Charlie, Barney, Maui, Fluffy, and Sheba.

Special purrs of gratitude to my wonderful editor, Deirdre Mullane (and her cats, Spot & Dot), kind agent, Carole Abel, and Croton neighbor, Jerry Gross.

Last but hardly least, many thanks to illustrator Larry Ross, for turning all our work into play.

CONTENTS

Contents

Introduction

It is a sultry August morning in a small farming community in the Midwest. Abigail, a yellow tabby with sea green eyes, licks the last drops of cool milk off her pink nose, washes her paws and whiskers, and saunters out the catdoor to begin her daily rituals.

After locating a spot in the grass that's glowing with a vibrant green and yellow healing force, she settles in for a long, luxurious bath, which she follows with a head-to-tail aura cleaning and fluffing, a series of meowed affirmations intended to heighten her sense of well-being, and a twenty-minute meditation in which she turns her attention away from the activities of chirping birds and scampering squirrels to focus on the sound of her own purr.

Abigail, and millions of cats all over the world like her, is responding to the call of a New Age, and on January 1, 2000 (with paws over ears to shut out the din), she'll welcome a new Millennium. Although most felines have little interest in linear time, the fact that the twenty-first century is almost under paw is something all cats can sense without counting up or down.

The signs are everywhere. A cat's simple credo of sleep, eat, and prowl has widened to encompass kitty consciousness-raising activities that include everything from divining the outcome of your day from the way the sand falls under your paws in the litter box, to rubbing against amethysts or rolling in a blend of Purrgamot and catnip to relax.

These days, even purring has a higher purpose. Ordinary catnaps have become times for out-of-furbody meanderings, lucid dream mouse hunts, or rendezvous with fluffy spirit guides. Even vacant staring into an empty mouse hole has become an opportunity for creative visualization, focused purring meditations, or, if you're gifted like the prophet Nostracatus, a way to see visions of what's to come.

Just sinking into your favorite human's lap for a little cuddle can become an enlightened, healing moment, by kneading along the right meridians, transferring heat and light, and connecting your Purr Chakra with the human Heart Chakra while you're laying on your paws.

As you enter this new age of enlightenment, a "catus

novus," or new feline, is beginning to emerge. In addition to becoming a fur-bearing satellite dish capable of picking up energy transmissions from all over the universe, you're shifting your attitudes. By moving toward a heightened spirituality, you're moving away from dog-eat-dog value systems, competition for the best spot on the sofa, and ferocious territorial purrsuits.

These signs of inner growth extend far beyond your own tail. You realize that Planetary Karma is like personal Kitty Karma. When you honor and respect the needs of Cat Mother Earth, giving her the grooming, petting, detangling and tender nurturing care she needs, you and all the creatures on the planet will reap the rewards.

What's next? Cat Mother Earth, and every swirling ball of energy in the universe, is bristling with change. Curl up with *A Cat's Guide to the Millennium* and take a peek under the door to the future.

ONE

Unseen Energies

A cat is a force field in a fur suit.
—Rampurr

When Daffodil, a bright golden longhair well-versed in New Age protocol, washes her coat, she spot-checks for blocked chakras as well as for fleas. Like more and more contemporary felines, Daffodil realizes that she's a frozen fur ball of swirling electromagnetic energy and is using all her senses to get switched on.

It hasn't been an easy path. When Daffodil was a kitten, her clairvoyant abilities were confined to sensing which laps were most hospitable, chasing after meddlesome ghosts or appuritions, forecasting storms, or enjoying an occasional romp with playful fairies or elementals under a full moon. Even Dusty, her gray tiger tabby dad, used to say: "Why chase mice in other dimensions when the three on this planet are trouble enough?"

Why? As we approach the Millennium, cats are finding that the unseen energies that whirl around their whiskers, ears, and tails can no longer be ignored. Worlds are merging. Feline frequencies are accelerating, and multidimensional games of cat and mouse are speeding up. The invisible is finally becoming visible.

To attain full Cat Consciousness you'll need to activate your energy systems, bathe often, and give your electrical field a thorough fluffing up.

The Cat Chakra System

Walking on the fence of life requires balance.
—Upurranisheds

Besides having a fur body, you have an energy body. The electromagnetic energy that swirls, pulses, and dances through you is known as your *purrana*, or life force. Your chakras are the circuits that move this energy around, and each chakra has a different function.

Kitty clairvoyants say chakras look like whirling bouquets of brilliant bird feathers, with varying amounts of plumage and coloration. When a chakra is running smoothly, they say it resembles a peacock in a fast tailspin.

When your Cat Chakra System is properly aligned, you can follow a squirrel out onto a delicate branch and not lose your balance, but when your chakras are blocked, the squirrel gets away and you fall.

Chakra malfunctions are the cause of everything from lackluster fur to being hissed at by members of the opposite sex.

A good paws-on practitioner will use crystals, visualization, and bodywork techniques that can not only open up your chakras but change your life.

There are nine cat chakras.

The Petting Chakra. Placed between the ears, this chakra rules cat spirituality, out-of-body travel, and being petted. Petting is a powerful two-way energy transmission that raises the frequencies in both the petter and the pettee. Humans receive tremendous health benefits through the Petting Chakra, experiencing lowered blood pressure and a sense of inner peace. Cats with blockages in this chakra will typically butt their heads against the furniture and require extra petting. Chakra color: ultraviolet.

The All-Seeing Eye. This chakra is located in the middle of the forehead, right between the ears. (On tabbies, it's found right under the M.) The All-Seeing Eye allows you to see in the dark, see what's for supper, see appurritions, and see the past, present, and future simultaneously. (The Egyptian Eye of Morris is a symbol for this chakra.) Chakra color: purple.

The Meow Chakra. Located in the throat, the Meow Chakra is the seat of expression and empowers you to make specific demands with regard to meals. It also rules clairaudience (eavesdropping on the spirit world), and simultaneous translation (understanding what other species have to say). Most Siamese have an overly active Meow Chakra, while that of soft-voiced Persians tend to be blocked. Chakra color: blue.

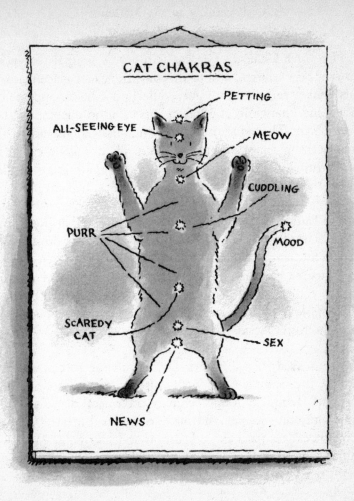

The Purr Chakra. The cat is the only animal that possesses a Purr Chakra, and to this day, the exact placement of this chakra remains a mystery. The Purr Chakra appears to move and change in size, often appearing to encompass the whole body. This conduit for love and bliss can also act as an anesthetic in times of stress or pain. High angelic essences enter through this chakra, with a loud, rumbling purr indicating their presence. Chakra color: pink.

The Cuddling Chakra. This chakra is located at the heart, and when fully opened radiates waves of loving warmth that can be felt across an entire room. Sweetness, snuggling, rubbing heads, touching noses, bathing a friend, and similar cuddly cat behavior flows from this chakra. It also rules maternal love. An overactive Cuddling Chakra produces lap cats who won't let go. Chakra color: green.

The Scaredy-Cat Chakra. Located in the soft pit of the tummy, the Scaredy-Cat Chakra filters sensitive feelings and accounts for finicky feline behavior. Likes and dislikes, emotions, unresolved fears, and memories of bad meals are held here. Blockages produce indigestion and hair balls. "Yellowbellied" cats who display the "Scaredy-Cat Response" (fight or flight) need work in this area. Chakra color: yellow.

The Sex Chakra. This chakra, located near the base of the tail, is where sex play starts. A cat with a blocked Sex Chakra can turn into a pugilistic bully who marks the whole town with his scent. Sex Chakra energies can be used for procreation, catting around, or creativity. Excessive activity in this chakra accounts for why, after a night of romantic liaisons, some toms still croon for more. Chakra color: orange.

The News Chakra. Tucked right under the tail, the Information Chakra functions as a twenty-four-hour news station that provides current updates on a cat's disposition, health, and desires. When members of the same species need personal information, they check in here. Energy readouts from this chakra will draw some cats closer and keep others at bay. Chakra color: red.

The Mood Chakra. The feline tail has a mind of its own, and the Mood Chakra functions as a regulating device. Located at the tip of the tail, the Mood Chakra gets rid of excessive static electricity and helps cats answer simple "yes" or "no" questions like: "Should I go or stay?" Incessant tail flipping is a sign of blockage in this chakra. Color: silver.

The Care and Cleaning of Your Aura

Beauty is only fur deep.
—Persian proverb

Feline beauty doesn't stem from a shiny fur coat. What makes one cat more radiant than another is the life force, or purrana, they emit, and the quality of their aura. Any cat who wins best in show undoubtedly has an aura that's as pleasing as its face.

The aura is an egg-shaped envelope of electromagnetic energy, with constantly changing colors and shapes, that reveals a feline's emotional and mental states.

All cats have the ability to see auras but switch it off because it interferes with their naps. But with the onset of a highly charged Aquarian Age, cats will be relying on this special gift of sight.

Stronger Than Scent

To find out who you're touching noses with, size up their aura. A cat's pedigree, breed, astrological sign, or scent won't begin to reveal as much about its health, character, or degree of spiritual development as its aura can!

In the normal course of life, particles of your aura get sloughed off like cat dander, leaving an electromagnetic trail for anyone to follow. This aura dander is what leads police dogs to culprits and reunites pets with families who've moved on. Aura dander also magnetizes everything you frequent, imbuing your favorite blanket or pillow with a frequency that's yours alone. This allows cat clairvoyants to perform highly revelatory readings by using your cat collar, or a favorite toy, even if you're not present.

What Color Is Your Aura?

Your aura is colored by the life you lead. Everything you think and do affects the way it looks.

For example: Let's say you've had a tiff with a Persian neighbor and venomous thoughts of sinking your claws into her fluffy white back begin to cross your mind. Harboring these hateful feelings will turn your aura *black*. If you're jealous of her, and covet her soft, luxurious lifestyle, your aura may turn a vile shade of *green*.

What if she comes at you first, ears back, tail bristling, teeth bared, and snarling fiercely? If you're consumed by fear, your aura will turn a pallid *gray*. But if you get mad and decide to attack, your aura will be bright *red* and flashing—STOP!

If pride gets in your way, it may turn your aura *orange*. But if you sit back on your paws and think things through with a clear mind, your aura could turn a pretty shade of *yellow*.

Say you decide that since you're neighbors, you'll try to be friends. This loving feeling will engender a lovely *pink* hue. Even if she doesn't see your pink aura, she'll feel it and respond in a favorable way, leading to nose-touching reconciliation. Such sweet behavior could transform both your auras into a beautiful, soft shade of *blue*.

Cleaning Your Aura

Just as your fur needs frequent cleaning, so does your aura. A messy aura is a nasty sight. The colors look dingy. The lights are dull and dim. There are spots, streaks, and turbulent swirls. Even if you can't see it, you can feel it, and it's worse than a bad case of static fur.

One of the best ways to clean your aura is to give yourself frequent baths. For a complete cleaning try the following technique on yourself, or swap aura cleanings with a friend.

Shake Out Your Fur. Starting at your ears, vigorously shake your entire body, so your fur gets magnetized and fluffs out.

Magnetize Your Paws. Place one paw over the other, not touching, and slowly move them back and forth until you feel the energy build up between them and become dense.

Paw-Scan Your Aura. Close your eyes. Hold your paws several inches away from your fur. Slowly paw-scan your body—feeling for where your aura is electrically matted or tangled.

Dry Cleaning. In places where your paws pick up dense, sticky, or hot energy, pull off the static snarls and deposit them in a plant. (Plants like to eat static and come to no harm.) Do this all over your body until your aura feels smooth and cool.

Aura Fluffing. Give your newly cleansed aura an overall fluffing with your claws, feeling the air for areas that still feel snarled and tangled, directing the energy up toward your ears. Lie down to fluff your tail, allowing yourself to drift off to sleep.

Kitty Kundalini

The energy of all creation sleeps in the tip of your tail.
—The Dharmapurrdmeow

Something odd is going on. An invisible power, known as Kitty Kundalini, is waking up and causing cats to behave strangely. You see things you never saw before, or spot small changes in yourself. An unassuming tom who's out for a midday stroll suddenly stops in his tracks and breaks into a little flip. A quietly meditating Burmese floats several inches up in the air. In a meadow, you notice circles of cats whirling and twirling on their tails, and their spinning bodies emit a blue glow.

Then one afternoon your own whiskers start to itch and vibrate like a tuning fork, and your tail begins to quiver. This sensation is so pleasurable that you completely forget to have dinner, and when it's over, you're somehow transformed. These are signs of the changing times and examples of the Kitty Kundalini awakenings that cats all over the planet are presently experiencing.

Kundalini is an ancient Catskrit word for the powerful, transformative energy that lies curled up in a ball, like a sleeping kitten, at the tip of your tail. When your Kitty Kundalini is aroused, it climbs up through all nine chakras, causing all sorts of unusual sensations as it travels. When it finally reaches your Petting Chakra, it flows out through the space between your ears.

When your Kitty Kundalini is fully activated, you operate in peak pussycat condition, with all your channels open and receiving. Paranormal feats become normal when this energy's engaged. But it takes time. It's harder to wake up than your human on a Monday morning, and can require more than nine lives. Here are some exercises to get it going.

WARNING: Do these exercises slowly. Releasing your Kitty Kundalini too rapidly is not only perilous, it's as unpleasant as being abruptly jolted out of a deep catnap.

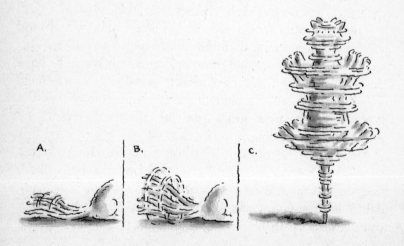

A.   B.   C.

Kitty Kundalini Activators

Tail Flips. To begin awakening your Kitty Kundalini, focus on your tail and do slow, rhythmic flips—back and forth, back and forth. Work up to an hour of flips a day, increasing your speed as you progress. When your tail begins to tingle, move on to the next exercise.

Tail Twirls. Visualize the Kitty Kundalini energy as a thread of golden light running from the tip of your tail to the top of your head. Whirl your tail in small concentric circles, increasing the size of the circles as you feel the energy rise.

Tail Spins. When the energy is finally aroused, it's enough to blow off your whiskers. Exercise extreme caution. Begin tail spinning close to the ground, sitting on your haunches. After some flipping and twirling warm-ups, your tail will begin to tingle and vibrate, and your fur will bush out. Then, in a flash of light, you'll be up on your tail in a spin. Each spin will raise your vibration higher and higher, eventually connecting you with All That Is.

WARNING: Overspinning can send you soaring straight out of your body. Focus on a food you like and attempt to wind down.

Good-bye Hiss. As the Kitty Kundalini energy travels from the tip of your tail to the top of your head, your lower animal nature will get traded for your higher animal nature. It's good-bye hiss and hello bliss. You'll see the world, and your role in it, in a whole new way.

Currently the Kitty Kundalini in most felines is on the rise. This means that Cat Consciousness is expanding and no kitty will ever be the same. Just be aware: Once you start spinning there's no going back. If you don't feel you can handle the energy, or like things the way they are, put your head under the pillow, tuck in your tail, and let that "sleeping kitten" lie.

TWO

Connecting with Your Higher Cat

Heed the voice that meows from within.
—Lao Tzu Paws

Cat masters warn us that material comforts and catnip-infused diversions of twentieth-century life are traps set out to lure overly coddled pussycats away from the spiritual path. They recommend connecting with your Higher Cat, who sees in the dark better than you do and knows where the path is full of thorns. Just where, you may be wondering, does your Higher Cat curl up and how do you connect?

Meditation, which is not to be confused with catnapping, is one of the time-honored ways. Your Higher Cat is always near you, but needs an empty channel to be heard. By shutting out distractions and clearing unnecessary fluff from your mind, you can tune into his or her wise meows.

Crystals will also help you connect. If you've been resenting the fact that they sit in spaces you might better occupy, it's time to make friends. You can start by giving these extra-ordinary mineral allies a therapeutic daily rub. Besides providing you with a good scratch, you'll find they make enlightening company.

Cat Aromatherapy is yet another way. This allows your Higher Cat to speak to you through your sense of smell, twitching your whiskers or wrinkling up your nose.

We'll explore them all.

Taming the Feline Mind

The undisciplined feline mind is like a dog chasing its tail. It keeps moving but goes nowhere.
—Meowharishi Meowhesh Yogi

As planetary forces speed up, you need to find ways of slowing down. Catnaps are one answer, but meditation is another. A cat with a quiet, focused mind is capable of preserving its life force, or purrana, and adding years to his or her nine lives.

Far Eastern felines, like the Siamese, Burmese, Persian, and Japanese bobtail, who have been practicing meditation for thousands of years, are adept at seamlessly flowing in and out

of meditative states—while Western cats find it easier to enjoy short, focused bursts of meditation, maybe twenty or thirty times a day.

Regardless of the techniques you use, some basic guidelines apply. First, be fully present. If you'd rather be cleaning the last morsels off your plate or investigating an empty box in the basement, you're not in the right frame of mind. Secondly, relax. No matter where you are, whether it's on the roof or under the sofa, find a position you can hold for a long period of time without losing your footing or dozing off. Thirdly, suspend all judgments about the process, or yourself.

Telling yourself things like "I have a kink in my tail and it's getting worse" or "The dog is watching me and thinks I'm an idiot" or "Fluffy's probably eating my dinner right now" will only make it harder.

Meditation Techniques

TM (Transcending Meals). This highly popular technique was first brought to the West by a famous Indian longhair known as the "Meowharishi." He discovered that cats have trouble meditating because their minds are constantly being distracted by thoughts about food. Being in the "now" is impossible when your mind's on the next meal. The object of

TM is to Transcend Meal preoccupation so meditation becomes possible.

To facilitate this, each cat is given its own meow sound, or mantra. These meow mantras have great power. Whenever food-related reveries creep in, simply focusing on the meow mantra will separate you from thoughts of your dish.

If you don't like your personal meow mantra, you can always chant *Yummmm*, the sound of creation, or the Tibetan shorthair favorite, *Yum Meowie Pet Me Yum*.

Research has shown that frequent Transcending Meals meditators tend to trim down effortlessly, are as pleased with the prospect of canned tuna as they are with fresh crab or sole paté, and enjoy an average of twelve or more lives.

There are also some TM offshoots of this type of meditation. *TS* is a highly effective rehabilitative tool for treating chronic furniture scratchers, and *TLC* seems to help itinerant bullies and runaway strays with low self-esteem.

Focused Meditation. Like staring at a blank wall or a dead bug, Focused Meditation is a mindless activity that's now been put to a smarter use. It doesn't matter what you focus on as long as it blocks out all distractions. You can even focus on your plate. This is called *conscious eating*. To do it, you bring your undivided attention to each aspect of your meal and label it. For example:

1. Sniffing the tuna
2. Pawing the tuna around on your plate
3. Placing the tuna in your mouth
4. Feeling the tuna on your tongue
5. Chewing the tuna
6. Noticing the tuna taste
7. Identifying the tuna (white, chunky, or albacore?)
8. Swallowing the tuna
9. Taking another bite

Mindful Purring. This popular technique calms your mind by having you focus on your purr. Not only does Mindful Purring carry you into a tranquil, meditative state, it produces a profound residual effect, raising the frequencies of all those who come within your range.

You begin with a soft, steady rumble. When your mind wanders, just return to your purr. Let one buzz roll into the next, like frolicking bees in the backyard on a hot summer day. Continue this meditation even when you're being brushed, petted, or cuddled. With practice, you'll feel like you're in a soft pink nest surrounded by the one Great Unifying Purr of Life.

Zen Kitty Koans. Zen cats, like Oriental shorthairs and Japanese bobtails, learn to meditate on Zen Kitty Koans.

Koans are questions that are impossible to answer with the rational feline mind. In the beginning, most cats either get a profound flash of insight, or fall fast asleep.

Zen Kitty Koans, like the following ones, help cats train their restless squirrel monkey minds.

What is the sound of one cat napping?
What is meow?
What did your whiskers look like before you were born?
Is sushi sushi or is it fish?
Why does cream have no bones?

The Mandala. A round symbolic design, resembling your dish, is called a Mandala. Focusing on its center helps you center within yourself, gets your mind off mundane pursuits, and often leads to insights on the interrelatedness of all life. Most cats know the Yin/Yang Mandala, which contains a black and a white cat. The most famous of all Mandalas were created by twelfth-century Tibetan tabbies. The treasured Cat and Mouse Mandalas depict the cosmic chase that never ends, and hang in museums around the world. In one of these sacred works, a meditating aspirant curled up on a pink lotus cushion comes to the realization that it's wise to put your focus on the chase instead of on the catch because we all come up empty-pawed in the end.

Crystal Power for Cats

*Two Rose Quartz Crystals (tied together with silver string).
A pawful of catnip mixed with a pawful of rose petals. A
silver saucer of cream. Two tufts of your own tail fur (leave
outside your door under a full moon and he will come).*
—Persian love potion

Ruby is a bright red Persian who shares her sunny window
perch with a large collection of crystals. What began as an
uncomfortable relationship has turned into a special kind of
cat and crystal comradarie, now that Ruby has turned a furry
ear to what the rocks have to teach.

It is happening everywhere. Cats are communing with the
mineral kingdom, and the ancient crystal healing secrets from
the days of Catlantis are no longer a secret. Cats are using
crystals as chakra balancers, scratching posts, and static fur
relievers; while holistic veterinarians, paws-on healers, and
cat bodyworkers are prescribing crystals to cure everything
from a lackluster romantic life to a stubborn case of fleas.

Wandering "rock groups" of itinerant kitties have taken to
traveling around the globe in search of powerful rock forma-
tions and electromagnetic "ley lines" that will connect them
to the planet's inner purr.

Because of its highly charged vortexes, Sedona, Arizona,
has become a happy stomping ground for millions of tiny

feline feet. Cats are found everywhere—sashaying in and out of tourist shops, prowling through the underbrush in Boynton Canyon, and sunning themselves on the upper ledges of Bell Rock, gleefully rolling around in electromagnetic energy fields until their coats are the color of the red canyon dust. Sedona's growing New Age cat population claims that the vortexes amplify your purrapsychological powers, and can make even the simple act of washing your whiskers a peak experience.

This current cat craze for crystals—just where and when did it all begin? According to the great catnapping prophet, Edpurr Catsey, felines living in the great ancient civilizations of Cat-lantis and Lemewria were conversant with crystals. After a hard day of mousing, cats would stop into crystal healing temples. Eyes, aching from hours of fixed focus, and legs, cramped from being hunched in one position, were quickly revivified through treatment from the right stones. According to Catsey, most of ancient Egypt's cat population wore crystal healing collars, and sacred temple cats ate their Amon Ra Tidbits and Nile Fish Munchies from gemstone-encrusted plates.

For cats who once camped with the gypsies or slept with seers, there were always crystal balls. These spheres proved to be magical windows that could reveal the time and place of your next meal or the breed of Mr. Right. Because they rolled, they proved good for play, and on hot days, their smooth, cool, crystalline surface provided a soothing mineral rub.

In times past, cats have used crystals to balance their chakras, increase their flow of purrana, and stimulate Kitty Kundalini. But the greatest use has been in healing. Their ability to add to your animal magnetism and act as protective amulets or talismans is what makes crystals so popular today. Here's a basic guide for their use.

Energize Your Cat Food

Placing clear quartz crystals in your water bowl helps restructure the crystalline properties of the water and speeds up your spiritual growth. Swallowing the stone does not make the ritual more effective.

To drink in the healing rays of a particular crystal, simply place it in your bowl, leave it in the sun for twenty-four hours, and drink.

Dining on a plate that's gold, silver, or decorated with gemstones will aid digestion. If you're relegated to bone china, porcelain, or plastic, tuck a chunk of citrine under the plate.

Crystal Aids to Catnaps

Before dozing off lay out nine crystals that correspond to the nine Cat Chakras and sleep on top of them. This helps clear emotional blocks and improves the energy flow while you sleep. If it feels bumpy, put a soft cushion between you and the rocks.

To align yourself with the earth's electromagnetic field, sleep facing north. For better dream recall, place clear quartz crystals in all your favorite sleeping spots.

Give These Crystals a Daily Rub

Amethyst. Amethyst is a great spiritual purifier, healer, and tranquilizer. Its transformative powers can help even the lowest backbiting toms find their higher nature. If you've been out prowling all night or overimbibing in catnip, amethyst will ease your tired eyes and help you sober up. If you suffer from insomnia between catnaps, enjoy a good amethyst scratch right in the middle of your forehead. Your Petting Chakra benefits from a daily amethyst rub.

Clear Quartz. By enhancing the crystalline properties of the blood, body, and mind, clear quartz crystals can help you get rid of fleas or fur balls. To amplify your desire for an early dinner, just meow your request into the crystal and it will project the message to your human provider. To enhance communication with your Higher Self, cat spirit guides, and attractive toms, hang a clear quartz crystal from your cat collar. Give your All-Seeing Eye a daily rub.

Smoky Quartz. After a cat spat, or in times of stress, take a moment to brush by a smoky quartz crystal. It will calm you down. If you find yourself lusting after the Maine Coon who lives next door, find a large crystal and jump on it. This helps balance your Sex Chakra and dissipates negativity. If the day looks cloudy and you're in the mood for hot sun, gaze into a smoky quartz crystal and imagine the clouds going away.

Lapis Lazuli. Ancient Egyptian cats wore powerful carved amulets made of lapis lazuli, such as the legendary "Eye of Morris" seen in hieroglyphs. Rubbing your All-Seeing Eye against a chunk of lapis lazuli enhances your ability to view unseen worlds and navigate in the dark. Since lapis lazuli is an aid to self-expression, it's recommended for all Siamese who suffer from a blocked Meow Chakra. They'll find the blue color especially soothing to their eyes.

Rose Quartz. This "Love Stone" has the capacity to bathe you in feelings of softness, cuddliness, and reverence for All That Is. Apply it to your Love and Purr Chakras after a fastidious head-to-tail cleansing. Rose quartz is a natural hiss deactivator that clears away jealousy and resentments and promotes interspecies harmony. To attract a special someone, hang a small rose quartz crystal around your neck.

Pink Tourmaline. Because it dispels negativity and wards off biting insects, pink tourmaline is an invaluable aid to catnaps. This highly electromagnetic stone is also a natural healer that increases your sensitivity and sense of well-being. Cats who wear tourmaline on their cat collars purr with greater frequency, and according to Kirlian aura photography, emit a radiant pink energy.

Citrine. Yellow or golden citrine is good for calming the digestive tract and the emotions. Use it on your Scaredy-Cat Chakra if you feel queasy. To bring up fur balls or purge a bad meal, charge your water with citrine and lap it up fast. Citrine can also be used to quell excessively destructive tendencies, like couch shredding. Curling up with citrine is a warming, vitalizing activity that aligns you with your Higher Cat.

Amber. Amber, and especially specimens containing tiny fossilized insects, will help you focus on what's "bugging" you. Simply stare into the stone until the answer is revealed. Amber has the power to show you where you're "stuck" so you stop digging in your claws and let go. It also alleviates static fur cling. To calm the inner kitten hiding in your Scaredy-Cat Chakra, look to amber's balancing golden rays.

Carnelian. This gem is one of the most potent energizers known to felines, affecting the Kitty Kundalini and causing it to rise. As an experiment, tie a small piece on the end of your tail and check your Mood Chakra. Does your tail flipping pick up dramatically? Do you find it easier or harder to make decisions? Carnelian also creates its own electromagnetic field. If you're a neutered female who's having trouble keeping howling tomcats away from the door, create a protective circle of carnelians and sleep in the center.

Garnet. When your Information Chakra's on overload, hunker down over a piece of garnet. Sitting on red garnet clears your channels, unscrambles your frequencies, purifies the body, and regenerates the blood. Cats who are bullies should spend a lot of time crouched over garnets, as they help your lower animal nature seek a loftier means of expression.

Tiger Eye. Throughout the ages, cats have used this mysterious shiny brown stone to avert the "Evil Eye" and develop courage. Worn as an amulet, it helps cats see with the "eyes of a tiger," learning to always sniff first and never judge a cat by its stripes or spots. Timid tiger tabbies will get a boost from this character-building stone.

Treat your quartz crystals like good friends. Rub them with your head. Roll around with them. Place them on a part of your body that needs healing. Wear them as amulets on your collar. Hide them in places you frequent. Play with them for fun.

As the earth energies grow more intense, curl up with your crystals to stay balanced and calm. Crystals are always happy to serve you. They'll reveal their secrets and listen to yours.

Nosing Around in the New Age: Aromatherapy

*Let your nose be your guide while your whiskers
point you in the right direction.*
—The Korat

When you were first born, you and your littermates couldn't see or hear but you could smell. This is how you learned to distinguish between your mother, mothballs, and the dog.

Later on you learned to read with your nose. Sniffing out "pheromones" (substances that carry personal odors) helped you stake out your territory and find suitable dates.

You discovered that your nose connects you to the planet, directs you to your litter box, tells you which humans to trust, and that every new event is accompanied by crashing waves of nasal stimuli that help you survive.

Thousands of years ago your feline ancestors were assaulted with scents that differ from the ones you encounter today. Ancient Egyptian and Greek cats were forced to share their beds with humans who slathered themselves in overpowering perfumes, unguents, and oils.

The cats of ancient Rome had it even worse, as the Romans doused everything with fragrance—from their hair and bodies to their togas, beds, and walls of their homes. In simple defense,

Aromatherapy was embraced by the Roman cat masses around this time. Special fish oils, personal musky blends, and aromatics were used after baths, before bed, or after a night out on the Appian Way. As usage became more common, highly prized extracts were put to use by paws-on healers. Throughout history, Aromatherapy has provided felines with a means of preserving their own scent identity during especially pungent times.

Favorite Pussycat Potions

Today, cats are applying the principles of Aromatherapy for both mundane and lofty purposes; using oils, herbs, bark, flowers, fur, feathers, and musky elixirs as relaxers, aphrodisiacs, pain relievers, stimulants, aids to the digestive and respiratory systems, or as scented unguents that will improve the strength and sheen of your whiskers and coat. With an aroma lamp you can even inhale the vapors of potent herbs and oils while you catnap or enjoy a meal. Here are some combinations you might try:

NOTE: All animal scents listed are derived from natural oils rubbed from the fur of happy, living animals in natural ways.

A Walk on the Wild Side
(as stimulating as a stroll through the jungle)

Catnip extract	3 drops
Tiger musk	2 drops
Leopard musk	1 drop
Sandalwood	2 drops

On a Pink Cushion
(as calming as a snooze on your favorite pillow)

Pyrrh	4 drops
Frankincense	3 drops
Rose	2 drops

Bliss in the Kitchen
(stimulates the appetite, especially in finicky eaters)

Salmon oil	3 drops
Tuna oil	2 drops
Red snapper oil	2 drops
Catnip	6 drops

The Cream Bath

Cleopatra's cat popularized the scented bath, which follows a regular tongue bath. Cats who take to water, like the Turkish Van, will dive right into a cream bath, but for most other cats it may be paws first. Cream, a natural emulsifier, helps prevent dry fur, and for Persians who get matted, it helps detangling. Mix 10 to 15 drops of catnip oil into 3 to 4 tablespoons of sweet cream, pour into the tub, and crawl in.

Collar Sachets

One of the best ways to use aroma is to wear it in a small silk pouch attached to your cat collar. Scented sachets can be used to attract or repel, balance your aura, heal, and protect you while you get on with your life. If you're a tom trying to advertise your charms to the neighborhood ladies, you might try a drop of your own musk, mixed with two drops of panther or jaguar essence, in a catnip herb base.

For strays in search of loving homes, a sachet of rose petals, lavender, and ylang-ylang is said to invite pettings and lead to warm beds.

Felines trying to ward off aggressive bullies or mangy suitors in order to lead a quiet, contemplative life will find all the seclusion they seek by wearing a mixture of diffused skunk oil, citronella, and cinnamon bark.

Aromatic Paw Balms

Because you're four-legged, your paws don't get much time off. These soft, furry sensors are capable of high-level healing work and deserve special attention. Paw pampering begins with manicured claws. Humans handy with nail clippers, a scratching post, or tree bark can help. As you'll discover in paw reflexology, paws are the pathway to your overall health and well-being. Aromatic paw balms work wonders for pussy-cats with frazzled nerves and aching feet. If it's summer, having a cooling scented unguent rubbed on your paws and claws is sure to refresh.

Paws & Reflect
(a soothing, balancing, bracing balm to use after a prowl)

Angelica	4 drops
Sage	3 drops
Menthol	6 drops

Lemongrass	1 drop
Lawn grass	two pawsful

Special Treatments

If you're interested in rapid personal growth, caring for your whiskers is key. Besides weather sensing and helping you navigate under lawn furniture at night, these highly tuned antennae can hook you up to other dimensions when they're well oiled. If your whiskers become too dry or brittle they can't bend and rotate and run the risk of snapping off. Try a whisker massage oil. Find a basic oil you like, like salmon or shrimp oil, with several drops of a potent insect repellent like eucatlyptus blended in.

To keep your fur coat from losing its sheen, apply sweet almond oil right to your fur, or try an Aromatic Roll, like the two that follow.

Purification Roll in the Grass
(detoxifies and connects you with Cat Mother Earth)

Vigorously roll around in this mixture, and follow it with a bath.

Purrgamot	3 drops
Cedarwood	2 drops
Catnip	2 pawsful
Pine needles	1 pawful
Unscented kitty litter	1 pawful

Bengali Power Roll
(invigorating tonic, overall body strengthener)

Before territorial expansion or a night of conquests, roll in this recipe and yowl.

Tiger musk	8 drops
Catchouli	2 pawsful
Catnip	1 pawful
Curry powder	dash

 # THREE

Beyond Nine Lives

Although your cat suit is only a rental, treat it well.
—Depurr Chopra

Paws-on healing, cat yoga, feline bodywork, nine-lives extension courses, and past nine-lives regression sessions are presently garnering more attention than free cans of tuna. The mind/furbody connection has been made and pussycats are eager to control how they'll live, how long they'll live, and where they'll be reborn.

Today's cats want to create their own reality. Although the halcyon days of ancient Egypt offered moments to contemplate life after nine lives, the pressure to behave like a fur-bearing deity caused a fair amount of stress. In the Far East, while common cats moused for a living, pampered temple cats perfected many of the paws-on healing techniques we still use today. These teachings have recently been unearthed and are quickly filtering into the mainstream. As a result, ordinary cats are currently living longer, healthier lives.

Fur Bodywork

A kink in the tail means a kink in the emotions.
—Tiger Rough

Awareness about the feline body is growing, and most of you now realize that your body is a storehouse of information, and everything you ever did or thought or felt is recorded there. You also know that some of the more painful events, like the time you got locked in the closet or spun around by your tail, are cause for current aches and pains. Fur Bodywork can help.

A Fur Bodyworker can watch the way you slink through the hall or pounce on a ball and see where you carry the weight of emotional trauma or psychological upset. Massaging, manipulating, kneading, and paw-poking the body in the right places will improve your physical, mental, and spiritual health. Cat yoga will help you maintain it. Through Fur Bodywork, you can begin to release the past so you'll be happier in the present, and better prepared for the onsetting times.

Chatzu is an ancient Oriental shorthair healing art that employs paw-poking techniques. It was introduced to the West by a Japanese bobtail with a black collar in katrate. According to Chatzu, there's an energy flowing throughout

Felinedom called Kitty Chi. When your Kitty Chi is blocked by injury or a poor lifestyle, you show the symptoms.

The Chatzu practitioner uses his or her front and back legs, all four paws, and head to apply body pressure along all the catupressure points in order to stimulate the Kitty Chi and relieve whatever ails you.

Catupressure is a similar technique. Here, the paws poke deeply into the fur in order to stimulate key catupressure points. This unblocks Kitty Chi and promotes self-healing. For cats with an uncontrollable tendency to bite or scratch any paw that pokes them, it's not recommended.

There are many forms of cat *massage*, although Swedish Forest Cat massage techniques are the most famous. Here, the paws knead, stroke, tap, and pet the entire feline body. Massage provides such deep relaxation that most cats immediately fall asleep. The use of aromatic massage oils is best avoided, as they mat up the fur and take too much licking to get off.

One of the most therapeutic forms of cat massage is known as *Roughing*. Developed by a domestic shorthair named Tiger Rough, this technique helps release pent-up emotions and blocked memories. Rough kneading softens the deep connective tissues and connects you with past memories of similar rough treatment. You feel it, you remember it, you hiss a little, you cry a lot, you forget it, you move on.

CERTIFIED
ROUGHER

Tiger Rough identified a pattern of emotions relating to different parts of the body. Feelings of neglect from insufficient petting are related to chest tension; the upper back holds anger, which causes hissing; the jaws contain sadness, which leads to biting and nipping; and the tail carries confusion. Roughers loosen up body parts you didn't even know you had, resulting in cats with better posture who carry their tails higher. First practiced at the Catsalen Institute in California, Roughing is famous for developing more structurally integrated, if slightly bruised, pussycats.

Today, millions of felines consider *catropractic* bodywork vital to their well-being. For many, the catropracter, who realigns the spine through gentle manipulation, has replaced the vet. The theory is that a properly functioning nervous system promotes good health. A long stretch on the catropractic table also alleviates the little kinks that come from crouching next to mouse holes or sleeping upside down.

Cat yoga, with its many "catsanas," or yoga postures, was first brought to the West by a group of sleek and agile Bombay and Bengali followers of Swami Purrananda. Today cats all over the world practice daily sun and moon salutations, pussycat stretches, and purranayama breathing exercises to increase their purrana, or electrical current, by turning up the voltage. Those who yearn to push way beyond the languid morning wake-up stretches are discovering that Pussycat Power Yoga, with its rigorous tail twists, has its rewards.

Laying on of Paws

Being four-legged gives you twice as much
healing power in your paws.
—Swami Purrananda

Although all cats have healing power in their paws, some have a real calling. Born healers are easy to spot. They can literally "hear" through their feet and have bright bands of electromagnetic energy around their fur. As kittens, they tuck their unusually hot little paws under their bodies while they sleep, groom their nails frequently, and flee from manicures. If they get into scrapes they just apply their paws to the wounds and heal in no time.

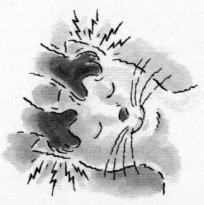

Mittens' Amazing Mittens

Extraordinary paws-on healers still make the news. *The Cat Times* was the first to print the story of Mittens Westerlake, now one of the country's greatest feline healers. In June 1991 Mittens' mother reported:

A male from my litter came in the other morning with his right ear badly torn from a fight. Young Ruggles was a sorry sight! Mittens, my four-month-old calico, scampered over to where he'd collapsed, lay down beside him, and placed her two white paws on his head. I thought she was picking a bad moment to play. I left them alone and went to the living room sofa for my morning catnap. When I returned, I saw something remarkable: Ruggles' ear was completely healed.

Kirlian photography subsequently revealed that Mittens had a visible force field, with an unusual pattern of flares, around her mittens. She went on to heal pets, plants, and people, laying her amazing paws on everyone and everything in need.

Paws of Light Healing Techniques

Whether you decide to use your paws on yourself, on others, or in Paws of Light healing circles, you'll find their ability to soothe, heal, redirect energy, and rebalance auras is astonishing. Here are some basic techniques:

Your First Kneads. As a kitten, you learned to transfer healing energy as you nursed, kneading your mother with your tiny paws. Kneading got you dinner and helped your mom get back on all-fours. Recall this feeling as you knead someone or something that gives you the same warm feeling as your mother.

The Knead to Heal. Choose an agreeable subject and curl up beside it. Magnetize your paws, as you would for an Aura Cleaning, rubbing them back and forth until you feel tingling, heaviness, or heat. Locate your subject's chakras, determine which are blocked, and knead on those areas until you detect changes in temperature (cooling) or electrical force.

Lap Energy Transfer. Curl up on your subject's lap and activate your Purr Chakra. Send healing energies into their body as you purr. Begin to knead. If the subject complains that you're shredding their clothes and tries to push you off their lap, postpone your treatment.

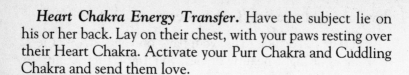

Heart Chakra Energy Transfer. Have the subject lie on his or her back. Lay on their chest, with your paws resting over their Heart Chakra. Activate your Purr Chakra and Cuddling Chakra and send them love.

Paws-on-Head Healing. Place your paws on either side of the subject's head. (This can be done while your subject sleeps.) Tap into your Higher Cat or Kitten. Direct your healing energies, along with any specific meal requests, into their heads.

Snoozing White Light Transfer. Curl up with a furry friend. As you doze off, embrace each other with your paws and visualize healing white light penetrating each other's fur coats.

Shakti-Pet. In this technique one spiritually developed cat enlightens another by giving them a special pat on the head. This pat is called "Shakti-Pet" because it wakes up the "shakti," or Kitty Kundalini at the base of your tail, causing a surge of transformative energy to be released throughout your entire body.

Rei-Kitty: Paws-on Healing from the Orient

You've got the whole world in your paws.
—Master Pussyui

Rei-Kitty, which taps into the Universal Life Force Energy (also known as "purrana," "Chi," or "Kitty Ki") is presently a paws-on favorite in the feline healing community because it allows you to use your own paws to heal yourself.

This natural healing method, which is thousands of years old, was rediscovered by a Japanese bobtail named Mikao

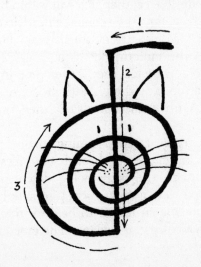

Pussyui in the 1800s. After digging up some sacred Catskrit scrolls long buried in Tibet, Pussyui discovered many incredible laying-on-of-paws techniques that he was empowered to use on his own aching paws and broken, ragged claws.

Crawling back down the mountain after his long, arduous dig, Pussyui discovered he could also heal others, effortlessly removing the fleas, healing the scrapes, and easing the pains of the Tibetan pussycats who gave him sustenance along the way.

News of Rei-Kitty spread fast, and with freshly washed paws and some potent magic symbols that had been mysteriously revealed to him during a catnap, Pussyui was in business, healing and "attuning" cats so they could be Rei-Kitty masters too.

Today, finding a Rei-Kitty master is easy. Their cards are often posted on the bulletin boards at your veterinarian or bulk pet food store. For a fee, they'll even drop in on your own Kitty Kozy and attune you there! With proper instruction, you can be empowered to heal yourself or others using the same techniques.

During Rei-Kitty treatments, healing energy enters through the Petting Chakra and exits through the paws. You always use both paws, with the pads facing down and toes held together, as if you were going to scoop some kibbles out of a bowl. All you need is an intent to heal for the Rei-Kitty Ki energy to automatically start flowing. The moment you lift up your paws it stops.

Rei-Kitty is more than just a system for healing. Pussyui also brought us The Five Principles of Rei-Kitty to help us improve our spiritual lives. They are:

Just for today I will be grateful for whatever's on my plate.

Just for today I will not worry about what will be on my plate tomorrow.

Just for today I will not be angry about whatever's not on my plate today.

Just for today I won't think about what's on anyone else's plate.

Just for today I will show love and respect for all living things even when they're not feline.

FOUR

The Empowered Feline

Even the wishes of a flea reach to Heaven.
—Siamese saying

As we move toward the Millennium, most self-respecting felines refuse to search for self-esteem underneath the covers or on some human lap. You've realized that dependence on doting humans robs you of your power and dignity, and is also unreliable, since today's people are much too preoccupied to be good servants.

Enter the Empowered Feline, padding in on big cat feet, with less leaning on humans to survive. Closet Kings and Queens of the beasts, time to fluff up your ruffs and yowl for what's due.

If you're not empowered, it's time you were. You can start by examining the state of your Kitty Chi and making sure your litter box is correctly placed by brushing up on your cat Feng Shui. After that you can create a soft life with personal affirmations and a healthier life with positive thoughts. It's all a matter of mind over fur, and even the way you wash your paws after each meal or the direction in which you catnap can change your life.

Feng Shui for Cats:
The Tonkinese Art of Placement

A cat's position in life is determined by
where she chooses to curl up.
—Catfusious

Li Shou is a Siamese talk show purrsonality. When her ratings dropped she called in her friend Maui, a Tonkinese Feng Shui expert. The first thing that Maui noticed was that Li Shou's staircase ran straight down into the catdoor. According to the laws of Feng Shui, Li Shou's luck, her ratings, and her Kitty Chi were leaking out the door.

Creating a life with all the creature comforts is every feline's dream. To encourage good fortune, Eastern and Western felines, and most notably, Japanese bobtails, have turned to Feng Shui. Feng Shui is the ancient Tonkinese art of designing space so the energy, or Chi, flows in harmonious patterns, leading to a soft, cushy life.

Your Kitty Chi

Cat Chi is the force that links you with all of life. When it's blocked, you're blocked. Simple things like changing the placement of your litter box, hanging a bright fish mobile over your feeding area, or napping only in a spot that's kitty-corner to the front door can transform your life by causing the energy to circulate around you in a more beneficial way. Poor placement can destroy your love life, trouble your sleep, and make you an easy mark for fleas.

An Ancient Art

The first shorthairs to practice cat Feng Shui were inhabitants of China over three thousand years ago. Some of the more astute felines of the time noticed that having a protective mountain at your back would dissuade inquisitive packs of pandas from invading your territory and padding through your catnaps.

To find suitable spots for sleeping, perching, and courtship, highly revered Tonkinese geomancers were carried to the tops of mountains and blindfolded. To determine the path of the Chi, these fearless felines would curl themselves into balls and hurtle themselves down the hillsides, while attendants scurried to pick them up and place markers at the site of each crash. After subsequent tumbles from changing vantage points they were able to identify the fault lines on the mountains, and their bodies.

Over time, and after many nicked ears, cat Feng Shui experts learned to balance the five elements. With the sun on your fur, soft earth under your tummy, a metal bowl full of food, a wet stream to drink from, and the wood from a tree for filing your claws, life was good.

As the art and practice of Feng Shui spread, cats began vying for position. Pagodas were invented so that cats could perch by rank, with venerated pussycat elders commanding the topmost tiers. Eventually Feng Shui came west with migrating Oriental short-hairs, Burmese, Siamese, Tonkinese, and some basic rules of paw.

Situating Yourself in Nature

Before choosing any site, cats are advised to tune in to earth energies and feel the Chi. Land that resembles a feline profile is the most fortuitous. The ears should rise up behind you, like backrests, allowing you to settle on the forehead or muzzle portion of the snout, with a commanding view of nature, preferably a well-stocked stream, before you. It's best to avoid sites where you're lower than someone else unless they happen to be birds. To raise your Chi you can enjoy a quick roll in the leaves, or climb a tree.

Harmonious Homecomings

The entrance to your home sets the stage. If jagged rocks, overbearing weeds, and a broken skateboard stand between you and the catdoor, other obstacles may appear in your life. Your entry should be open and inviting. Do you travel along a gently meandering path that weaves through fragrant flower beds, or must you pass by two menacing stone lions before ascending a steep flight of stairs? Does a shut gate block your path?

Where is your catdoor located? If the back door is your front door, or a window is your door, or no door is your door because you're an outdoor cat, it affects your Kitty Chi. Ideally, your door faces south.

When you enter the house, what do you first see? If it's the litter box, then, like Pavlov's cats, you'll always jump in. If it's your dish, you'll always eat. But if you spot scratching posts, kitty jungle gyms, soft sleeping nests, piles of catnip toys and kitty teases, and a human who's eagerly waiting to entertain you, it's good Kitty Chi. A room that invites you to shift gears, relax, and play is ideal.

Is Your Kitty Chi Under the Bed?

To find out where the Kitty Chi travels and where it's stopped, experts use an energy Mandala called a "Ba-Gua" that can be applied to anything, from the home where you live, to the places where you sleep, to the position of your litter box or plate. By seeing where things fall, and what's missing from the picture, you can "cure" any imbalances with small Feng Shui

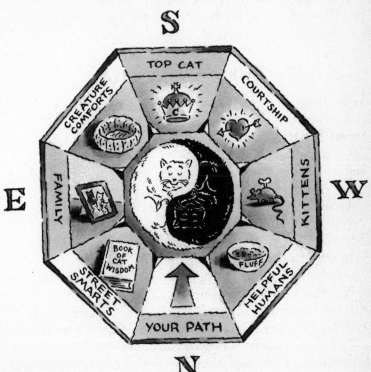

THE CAT BA-GUA

S

N

E

W

TOP CAT

COURTSHIP

KITTENS

HELPFUL HUMANS

YOUR PATH

STREET SMARTS

FAMILY

CREATURE COMFORTS

FLUFF

BOOK OF CAT WISDOM

tricks. To use the Ba-Gua, locate the position of your catdoor and orient yourself from there. Each section of your home should correspond to one of these categories, and what you find there will greatly influence these facets of your nine lives.

THE CAT BA-GUA

Your Path. Governs your direction in life, and if you're a working feline, your business or career.

Street Smarts. Governs how much you know and may come to learn.

Family. Governs your litter mates, the family pets, and your humans.

Creature Comforts. Governs all the factors that contribute to your good fortune.

Top Cat. Governs your territorial rights, status, and reputation in the neighborhood.

Courtship. Governs dating, mating, motherhood, devoted couplings, and cosy curl-ups.

Kittens. Governs your furry offspring and creative purrsuits.

Helpful Humans. Governs human benefactors who feed and care for you inside or outside the home.

Catnaps and Contemplation. Governs rest, meditation, and a search for wholeness depicted by the cat Yin/Yang symbol.

The Feng Shui of Harmonious Meals

There's good Feng Shui and bad Feng Shui, and if you want to enjoy mealtimes, stale negative energy is worse than two-day-old fish. If your food dish is positioned by a busy kitchen door and you must eat with your back to it, your digestion will be adversely affected and no matter what's on your plate, you'll walk away. If you're forced to take meals in a garage that's separated from the main house, you may feel disconnected enough to pack your catnip mice and move on.

For the best Kitty Chi your feeding area should be located in the Creature Comforts section of your house or kitchen, where ample and appealing choices of cuisine will be ensured. If it's not, try these Feng Shui cures. To deflect negative energy, place a mirror in front of your plate so you can see what's behind you while you eat. To absorb bad luck, stimulate your appetite, and be entertained while you eat, place an aquarium near your feeding area. Aquariums also foster prosperity, which can lead to second helpings and earlier or more frequent meals.

If you're in a multipet household that's mayhem around mealtimes, refuse to eat. Yowl plaintively, using your body to direct the can-bearing human to a secluded, serene corner spot with better Feng Shui.

Correct Litter Box Placement

Watch where you place your litter box! If it's in the Courtship area it's bad Kitty Chi. Symbolically, you'll be burying all your opportunities for romance. For better Kitty Chi, and a spotless litter box, move it to the section associated with Helpful Humans. If you lack privacy, hang a small crystal ball or a beaded curtain between your box and the disruptive energy.

The Ups and Downs of Feline Feng Shui

Always pick power spots that have a commanding view and don't let your tail face any approach. Positioning yourself where you can be stalked by another feline, surprised by a small child, or jumped on by a dog is dumb Kitty Chi. Never languish on open stairways, since energy, like sleeping cats, can fall through the cracks.

If you relish windowsills, pick a perch where the Kitty Chi flows up while you look down. Hang a cat flag, a wind chime, or a bird feeder to attract good Chi.

The Feng Shui of Sleep

For short rests and meditation, choose a spot in the Catnaps and Contemplation sector of your home. Auspicious spots allow you to monitor the traffic through your fur without having to open your eyes. If you're on a bed, never curl up with your paws facing the door, and always have your back to a wall, even when you're napping with a friend.

Check the condition of the spot where you sleep. Your nest sends subtle messages to your psykitty when it's in disrepair. A cat bed with a ripped pillow that leaks stuffing and a broken wicker frame will contribute to a feeling that you're coming apart at the seams and losing your resources. To encourage lucky dreams, rest your head on a red cushion or a ball of red yarn.

Never sleep facing a mirror. The Tonkinese believe that your soul leaves your body while you sleep, and if it sees its own reflection it will be confused and wake you up. (Another reason to avoid mirrors is the way you look with crumpled whiskers.)

The best Feng Shui rule of paw is to use your feline intuition and sleep around. By comparing different spots you'll be able to settle on the ones with the finest Chi.

Feng Shui Tips for Strays

There's an ancient Tonkinese maxim that states: "Good chi, good chow." Strays have the advantage of having a choice and are advised to frequent neighborhoods with fish-stocked ponds, bird sanctuaries, catnip gardens, and trout streams.

Streets with names like Fox Run Road, Coyote Crossing, Dogtrack Road, or Grizzly Bear Gulch are best avoided. A house that features cat knickknacks in the windows, a cat-motif mailbox, a Beware of the Cat sign on the lawn, and bird feeders in the front yard begs you to drop in for a bite.

Feng Shui and the Working Cat

Ever wonder why some cats enjoy kibbles and perks while others are always getting their tails stuck in desk drawers? If you're an office cat, where you choose to curl up determines your success in the job. If your tail faces the door, cat Feng Shui states that your paws will soon be hitting the street. If you face a window where a view of birds carries you into hunting daydreams, you may wake up in the unemployment line.

The best power spot is on top of a desk that's farthest from, and preferably kitty-corner to, the door. If you don't have a desk job, look for a position in the Top Cat or Creature Comforts section of the office, though avoiding the overstuffed red leather chair where the president sits.

Common Cures

Some favorite feline Feng Shui cures that increase or balance the Chi include using mirrors, dangling crystals on red cords, dangling catnip mice on orange cords, hot lights, wind chimes, aquariums, birds in cages, edible plants, cat statues, sphinxes, lion and tiger totems, large relaxation rocks in the sun, large bowls filled with kibbles, fish-filled fountains, whirligigs, mobiles, flags, peacock feathers, cat tease rods tied with red ribbons and placed at special angles, and auspiciously colored orange, red, yellow, green, or blue ribbons, yarns, fringes, tassels, and streamers that flap in the wind.

Among the typical kinds of problems easily cured with Feng Shui are:

Problem: Your catdoor faces in the wrong direction.

Cure: Placing catnip plants, red balls of yarn, lion statues, or wind chimes on either side of the catdoor will all correct the problem symbolically by redirecting the Chi.

Problem: Fluffy has usurped your preferred Feng Shui position on the side table under the Tiffany lamp.

Cure: Raise your authority and your Chi by climbing to a commanding site on the fireplace mantel and announcing it's your turn.

Problem: Noisy children and bickering adults sully the atmosphere in the Catnaps and Contemplation section of your home.

Cure: Clear the energy with sound. Put on a cat collar that's loaded with bells and race around the room.

To effect a Feng Shui cure cats use a ceremony that combines the power of speech, body, and mind by meowing a mantra nine times (like the Catskrit "Yum Meowie Pet Me Yum"), while holding their paws together in prayer and visualizing the objective.

FENG SHUI QUIZ FOR CATS

Your life and destiny are woven in with the workings of the Universe. Feng Shui helps you tighten any loose threads. Take this little test to find out where you need work and add up your score.

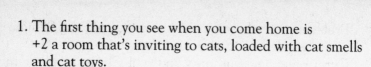
1. The first thing you see when you come home is
   +2 a room that's inviting to cats, loaded with cat smells and cat toys.
   −1 tools, sports equipment, children's toys.
   −2 your litter box.

2. Is your scratching post at the end of a long, dark hallway?
   −2 if yes

3. Can you see lush, green living things from your windows?
   +2 if yes
   −2 if no

4. Can you see a murky, stagnant pool of water from any of your favorite perches?
   −2 if yes

5. Are there any exposed ceiling beams above your food dish, litter box, or any of your perches or sleeping spots?
   −1 for each beam

6. Is your litter box in the kitchen? the basement? the garage?
   −2 if yes

7. Does your litter box get littered more than it gets emptied?
   −2 if yes
   −1 for each littered box in the house

8. Can you see the door from your favorite sleeping spots without having to twist your body in an uncomfortable forty-five-degree angle?
   +2 for each spot where you don't have to twist
   −2 for each spot where you have to twist

9. Does your catdoor swing freely on its hinges?
   +2 if yes
   −2 if no

10. Your favorite climbing tree is
    +2 on a hill behind your house.
    −2 directly in front of the entrance to your house.

11. The garage where you go for little getaways is
    +2 right next to basement.
    −2 across a swampy lawn at the end of a potholed driveway.

12. You and the other family pets
    +2 have separate sleeping arrangements.
    −2 are forced to fight for the same spots.

13. Your dining area is
    +2 on top of a round dining table.
    +1 in a private kitchen corner.
    −1 in a dark basement.
    −2 in the bathroom.

14. The bed you prefer to sleep on
    +2 is unoccupied.
    +1 is shared equally with your human(s).
    −2 is dominated by your human(s) every night.

15. Your house is next door to
    +1 a fish hatchery
    +2 a bird sanctuary
    −2 a Veterinarian

Scoring

+15 to +40. You have a harmonious environment that contributes to your well-being and gives you many reasons to purr.

+1 to +14. Happiness will be yours after you make a few minor adjustments by consulting a good feline Feng Shui expert.

0 to −45. Your Kitty Chi is being sapped by your environment. Make immediate alterations or move.

Creating a Soft Life: Affirmations

Dreams are the fluff that life is made of.
—Shakespurr

The words you meow and the pictures you see in your mind create your reality. Repeated often and with great conviction, they can take on form, so watch what you wish for! Every day, reaffurm who you are and what you've got. Even if you don't have it yet, act like you do, as it's part of the magic of affurmations. It's OK to want things, as long as there's still room on your plate. Just believe that the universe is abundant and eager to answer your requests.

Here are some of the more frequently used affirmations. Meowed loudly and often, they've been proven to work.

I am the highest order of animal on earth.
I deserve to be pampered.

The softest sleeping spots
are mine for the taking.

I am calm in a world of human chaos.

I need only my wits to survive.

My plate is forever full.

Fur balls are not a part of my life.

Life is a plate of fresh salmon.

I am loved for who I am no matter what I do.

My home is my temple.
Only goodness may enter in.

I scratch what I want when I want.
It is part of my nature.

I am master of the hunt.
Nothing escapes my grasp.

I bring my people presents and receive only praise.

I mark my territory well.
It is vast and it is all mine.

I am tougher and smarter than any cat on the block.

Plants are for me to eat, trees are for me to climb.
Life is good.

Humans shower me with toys.

My long, strong claws never need a trim.

I come and go as I please.
People love to open and close doors for me.

When I need to stretch in bed
my humans always make room for me.

Catnip is always mine for the taking.

The vacuum cleaner never disturbs my peace of mind.

I pick and choose all the family pets.

Hot sun is forever warming my fur.

Thunder and lightning pose no threat to my well-being
and never disturb my naps.

Laps are always mine for the taking.

Mind over Fur

*"Woundology" is looking for sympathy every time
you nick your ears.*
—Catlin Mice

Before there were vets, there were cats who knew how to heal themselves. Taking back the power begins with your own furbody, whiskers, paws, and tail. Through the groundbreaking work of cats like Louise Haykitty, Deepurr Chopra, and Catlin Mice, extraordinary information about the power of the feline mind over the feline body is becoming common knowledge.

The beliefs you have, and the thoughts you meow to yourself repeatedly, have a profound effect on your furbody. Negative patterns produce negative experiences and positive ones bring you joy. If you're willing to let go and forgive, getting rid of backbiting grudges and hissy resentments, almost anything can be healed.

Except for some carryovers from past lives, known as Kitty Karma, most ailments can be traced to your attitudes in this life. Anger, judgment, resentment, and guilt are the villains. Physical symptoms show up to enlighten you, and let you know where you're losing energy. They also tell you what kind of thinking needs to be fixed.

We've included several examples, showing the problem, the

way of thinking that may have contributed to it, and the affirmation to meow in order to heal. For a more complete reference, see Louise Haykitty's classic, *You Can Heal Your Fur*.

Problem: Catnip addiction.
Possible Cause: Running away from the self. Having one's tail stepped on repeatedly.
Thought to Meow: I may be small, but inside, I am big.

Problem: Free-floating anxiety. Hiding under beds.
Possible Cause: A basic mistrust of life.
Thought to Meow: I am safe.

Problem: Excessive appetite.
Possible Cause: Fear. A need of cuddling.
Thought to Meow: I am well loved.

Problem: Loss of balance.
Possible Cause: Not being centered in the self.
Thought to Meow: All is well with me.

Problem: Fur loss.
Possible Cause: Tension. Fear. Overgrooming.
Thought to Meow: I trust in life.

Problem: Fleas.
Possible Cause: Allowing others to get under your skin.
Thought to Meow: I am safe and secure.

Problem: Sensitive whiskers.
Possible Cause: Trouble facing life. Oversensitivity.
Thought to Meow: It's good to be me.

Problem: Tender paws.
Possible Cause: Unwilling to move forward in life. Not being grounded.
Thought to Meow: I am safe. The earth is my home.

Problem: Broken or splitting claws.
Possible Cause: Not wanting to let go. Having a grasping attitude.
Thought to Meow: I handle life with joy.

Problem: Fur balls.
Possible Cause: Fearing a loss of self.
Thought to Meow: There's only one me.

Problem: Throwing up on the living-room rug.
Possible Cause: Gut-level anxiety. Feeling disempowered over meal selection.
Thought to Meow: I will digest all new experiences joyfully.

Problem: Biting.
Possible Cause: Anger or mistrust.
Thought to Meow: Life is good to me.

Problem: Plaintive meowing.
Possible Cause: Feeling alone and frightened. A need to be heard.
Thought to Meow: I love and approve of myself.

Problem: Overgrooming.
Possible Cause: Self-rejection.
Thought to Meow: I am wonderful just as I am.

FIVE

Purrapsychology

There is only one journey: Crawling inside of yourself.
—Rilkitty

Slinking towards the twenty-first century with our collective tails between our legs, most of us display one or more symptoms of modern life, whether it's permanently flattened ears from harsh noise and shrill music, or the nervous claw chewing, overgrooming, overeating, and catnip abuse that come from being bored and left alone.

It's no wonder so many of us are currently seeing animal behavior therapists. What used to be called "destroying the furniture" or "using the carpet for a litter box" is currently referred to as "acting out." These animal behaviorists come to your home and study your every move, searching for clues, convinced there are deep purrapsychological motivations behind the way you scratch the arm of the sofa or knead the corner of the rug.

If you reduce the new baby's fuzzy pink lamb to a damp clump of chewed-up yarn, these cat shrinks blame it on sibling rivalry and suggest that your humans try buying you more toys. If you snarl every time someone tries to pick you up, it's not because you're nasty. It's because you were abused as a kitten or kicked as a cat.

If you're like most of today's "wounded" felines, you've found that having a problem gives you something to meow about in cat support groups and gets you more attention than yowling ever did. It also prevents you from being happy and whole. That's why there's purrapsychology.

This new discipline looks at what's really under your purr. By examining your cat psyche you can sort out your life. Through feline dream analysis, shadow work, the cat Enneagram (which explores personality types), or by accessing altered states, you can find your inner kitten, give it a good bath, and finally move on.

Feline Dream Interpretation

Dreams are the catdoor to the unconscious.
—Furreud

People wonder why cats sleep so much. You know the answer. It's in order to dream. Prowling around in the deep

psyche allows you to investigate those mysterious and normally hidden corners of your unconscious. The more opportunities you have to sleep or catnap, the more chances you have to dream. It's no wonder that in this supercharged time, dreams are every feline's favorite form of retreat.

According to Furreud, the German analyst who put cats on the couch, twitching whiskers, flickering eyes, and tiny mews mean there's an interesting show going on inside your head. Deciphering the veiled symbols that appear in your dreams takes practice. It's a bit like navigating around an unfamiliar neighborhood on a moonless winter night. But it was the famous Swiss shorthair, Cat Jung, who first noted that the same symbols appear, over and over again. We've included a glossary of these "feline archetypes" here.

There are many dream states. If you're an indoor cat, you might want to try something called "lucid dreaming." This is where you "wake up" while still inside your dream and begin to direct your dream's content, going anywhere your imagination will take you. You can fly like an eagle, stalk a sparrow, share a dream-time meal with Morris, or catch up with feline friends who've passed on. Some cats, well advanced in the art of lucid dreaming, have even managed to return from lucid dreams with actual prey. Whether they're symbol-laden dramas or wild, lucid romps, life is but a dream to an animal who spends 75 percent of its life asleep.

Here are some of the most common dreams and what they mean:

"I'm coughing up fur balls."
You're experiencing a deep unlayering of long-held beliefs about life that block your spiritual progress.

"I'm an actor in a cat food commercial."
This shows a desire for recognition and the need to be nourished on a grand scale, publicly.

"I dream that I'm a kitten playing with a ball."
Your inner kitten is yearning to find a means of expression. The ball represents a search for wholeness and integration between the kitten/cat sides of your psykitty.

"I turn into a bird and fly. Then I turn into a flying cat who swoops down and catches the bird."
You'd like to escape from the narrow confines of life but undermine your own chances for freedom with self-sabotage.

"I'm in a roomful of cats and have lost all my fur."
The opinions that other felines have about you is of prime importance. You feel stripped naked, unprotected, vulnerable, and chilly when your inner cat is on view.

"My human is gone. I'm in a empty apartment and my bowl is nowhere in sight."
Your dream is typical of modern "latchkey cats" who live alone and fear abandonment every time their provider leaves for work. It shows that you were snatched from your mother before you were fully weaned and continue to suffer from bouts of separation anxiety.

"Muffie, Slugger, and Mittens are giving me a bath. Their tongues lap at my fur and I feel content."
Your dream shows you still have infantile longings for your mother and never received the unconditional nurturing you needed as a kitten.

"I'm snoozing in a wingback chair."
Your ideas about comfort are highly traditional.

COMMON SYMBOLS IN CAT DREAMS

Actor: A desire for recognition. Your "role" in feline life.
Ball: Wholeness. Integration.
Bed: Rest. Retreat.
Bird: Freedom. Escape. The part of you that wants to fly.
Bridge: A transition.

Cage: Feeling trapped. Restrained expression.

Catdoor: Escape from an environment or situation.

Catnip: Wanting to change the way you feel. A desire to transcend.

Chair: Style. Attitudes and beliefs.

Chasing or being chased: The fears you're afraid to confront.

Closet: Identity. Where you hide yourself.

Collar: Feeling blocked or owned.

Dog: Obedience. Aggression. Stupidity. Masculine animal self.

Dark: The unknown.

Door: Access. A way out.

Eating: Pleasure. Nurturing.

Escape: Avoidance. Running from a feeling.

Falling: Insecurity. Humiliation.

Fleas: Minor irritation.

Fur balls: Unlayering of the self. Blockage. Being stuck.

Fur: Self-image. Protection. What you're covering up.

Home: The self. Where you reside.

Insect: What's bugging you?

Kitchen: Mother replacement. Nurturing.

Kitten: Infant self.

Lion: Deified feline archetype representing strength or courage.

Litter box: Memories of early litter box training, or the need to use one.

Littermates: Unexpressed aspects of your purrsona.

Losing something or being lost: Muddled inner sense of direction.

Milk: A need for mothering and nourishment.

Mouse: Fear of being insignificant, desire to dominate. Hunger.

Mouse hole: The unknown. Patience. Delayed gratification.

The number nine: Completion. Revelation.

Paper bag: The unconscious.

Paw: Self-expression, your grasp of life.

Scratching: A desire to get to the truth. Unlayering.

Stalking: A desire to discover or conquer. What are you looking for?

String: Attempts to unravel the mysteries of life. Amusement.

Veterinarian: Painful memories. Fear of being harmed.

Warmth: Cheerfulness, pleasure, love.

Washing: Getting rid of negative feelings and smells.

Water: Emotions. Fear of "getting wet" or feeling your feelings.

Window: Vision. A way out.

Finding Your Feline Shadow

A shadow that's been left in the dark for too long will bite.
—Buzzy Bliss

Every cat has a shadow. It's the flip side of your feline purrsona and usually the part you reject, deny, or disown. If you leave it in the dark for too long, it may jump out and nip at your feet when you least expect it. Learning how to spot it, accept it, and eventually make friends with it is the first step toward wholeness.

To find your shadow, don't look in your favorite places. Go where you can't stand the scent. Visit territory that's off-limits. If it makes you uncomfortable, it's where you need to be. Notice all the cats who make your fur stand on end. What is it about them that makes you want to hiss and duck behind the bushes? Are they too flea-ridden and foul-mouthed, too fluffy or fine-boned, too haughty or serene? When your ears flatten and your nostrils flare in disgust, you're encountering disowned shadow aspects of yourself. Sit quietly on your haunches and take a good look.

The following pairings are not atypical:

Marshmallow: A placid Persian who's forever preening her pristine white coat.
Spike: A battle-scarred, street-fighting tom who scent-marks everything in sight.

Musette: Scraggly, downtrodden tabby raising her tenth litter of kittens from another unknown father.
Princess Lu: Neutered lilac-point Balinese best in show with a broad vocabulary.

Caligula: High-strung Cornish Rex who dismisses most

brands of cat food by elegantly and disdainfully pushing them off the plate.

Mr. Goodfellow: Gregarious twenty-pound Maine coon who supplements his home meals with visits to several generous neighbors.

Learn to recognize your shadow. Shadow work puts an end to most hissy, antisocial behavior and will turn you into a more tolerant cat.

Remember, every cat and its shadow are only actors in a play. In your next set of lives, you may be the mangy one.

Purrsonality Types: Enneagrams

Your act gets you the tuna brand of your choice.
—Tigre Icatzo

One of today's most popular purrapsychological tools is the Enneagram, which lets you unlock the mysteries of your own purrsonality type and see why Fluffy's drives you up the fence.

Enneagrams were developed by a South American shorthair named Tigre Icatzo. His revolutionary map of feline behaviors

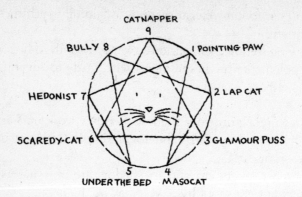

and motivations lets you understand the ways in which you interact with humans and other animals, and helps you uncover the games you play to get what you want.

Ennea is a Greek word for nine and *gram* means a drawing. In the Enneagram there are nine purrsonality types which fall into three groups of three.

The Feeling Triad
2. The Lap Cat 3. The Glamour Puss 4. The Masocat
The Doing Triad
5. Under the Bed 6. The Scaredy Cat 7. The Hedonist
The Relating Triad
8. The Bully 9. The Catnapper 1. The Pointing Paw

1. The Pointing Paw. Key Traits: Finicky to a fault, protests loudly when displeased, bathes often, destroys toys that don't meet the highest standards.

"Do you actually expect me to eat that?" Despite considerate gifts left on the doorstep, humanity remains insensitive to your needs. A hasty retreat from the dish, followed by a disdainful look, will let your humans know that they've failed you, once again. You asked for *Minced* Trout Supper, not flaked!

2. The Lap Cat. Key Traits: Possessive, flattering, digs into laps and won't let go, takes over most of the bed.

"Pick me up! Pet me! Cuddle me! Dangle the kitty tease in front of my face!" This seductive feline fatale will do anything for attention, like discreetly clawing the upholstered velvet chair to shreds as a statement of displeasure. Queen of sweet looks and soft purrs, you shed love and fur on anybody with a lap. And if someone's sick, you're there.

3. The Glamour Puss. Key Traits: Best in show or it's a hissy fit. Adores being groomed, flops down in the middle of social gatherings in order to be seen.

"Could someone fasten my rhinestone cat collar, please?" This type, who never lets you forget they were pick-of-the-litter, has mastered the art of the grand entrance. Hypnotic looks, fetching tail flips, and long, glamorous stretches on the casting couch often earn starring roles in movies and cat food commercials.

4. *The Masocat.* Key Traits: Sensitive, romantic, wails mournfully at the moon, has a weakness for catnip, highly creative with yarn, foil, and string.

"If only Mr. Fuzzball would wake up from his nap under the piano and notice me!" This long-suffering type is usually found curled up at the feet of struggling artists, or chasing recklessly after fleeting love affairs. Although you tend to choose a bohemian existence that encourages self-discovery, in your heart you yearn for a sensitive provider, a remedy for ear mites, and a clean litter box.

5. *Under the Bed.* Key Traits: Aloof, purranoid, absorbs scholarly nonfiction works through his fur, can flush the toilet, sleeps upside down, opens doors.

"Under here, at least no one pulls my tail." For this eccentric purrsonality type, life is a game of hide-and-seek. Because you enjoy an intellectual challenge, you hide everything you can get your paws on, including yourself, and prefer to take all of your meals, and most of your plunder, under the bed.

6. *The Scaredy-Cat.* Key Traits: Fearful, fur bristles from imaginary threats, bats at everything that moves, clings to human legs, habitually hides out deep inside a Pussycat Nest.

"It's a jungle out there and I'm no lion or tiger!" In your active feline imagination, someone's lurking behind every bush just waiting to pounce! Yes, you're a happy homebody, but you're also a nervous Nelly. Even a wide-open front door won't entice you to escape. You'd rather sit sentinel at the window and guard the family turf.

7. *The Hedonist.* Key Traits: Voracious appetite, disappears for days, stockpiles catnip toys, charming to neighbors who dispense treats.

"Why settle for half a can if you can wangle one or more?" You're a warm and cuddly con artist who believes life should be one long fabulous feast and are expert at finding people to indulge you. After you've sniffed out all the neighborhood's possibilities for pleasure, you promise to come home one morning and cover your people with loving licks.

8. *The Bully.* Key Traits: Territorial, battle-scarred leader of the cat pack, flattens his ears and fluffs up his fur to look threatening. His hiss is more dangerous than his bite.

"What's mine is mine and what's yours is mine too!" You'll dive-bomb them when they least expect it. Dominance is your

game. Woe to all pets who try to share your space, or your people. With tooth and claw you'll be victorious, even if it costs you a few tufts of fur and earns you a scolding.

9. *The Catnapper.* Key Traits: Indolent, sweet, easygoing, catatonic, a malleable mush who behaves like a stuffed, plush toy.

"Be sure to wake me so I don't miss my catnap." Your type is so laid back you run the risk of being mistaken for a rug. Children love to drag you around the house dressed up in doll clothes. When you knock over lamps, track in mud, or get trapped in the closet because you were half asleep, you're such a soft innocent that nobody minds.

Catnip Highs and Other Altered States

Opening the catdoors of perception only requires one sniff.
—Aldouspuss Huxley

Have you noticed? Feline lifestyles are undergoing dramatic changes. Without large territories to patrol, families to raise, or dinners to hunt up, it's easy to become bored, sedentary, and round. For diversion, cats are crawling into altered states, discovering that changing consciousness is as easy as changing positions on the bed.

New Age proponents of altered states argue that our normal mode of existence is too limiting, and although it suits our cat tribe to keep us in check, a leap into other dimensions is just the evolutionary jump-start we all need. Why not begin with a good roll in catnip?

Catnip

European and North American felines became aware of the mind-expanding powers of botanical plants way before their people, and *Nepeta cataria*, or catnip, has long been the herb of choice.

Recent studies have revealed some interesting facts about

catnip consumption: Only 50 percent of felines enjoy it, and the ability to get a buzz off of it seems to be an inherited trait. Another interesting fact is that not all users like to roll in it. Some are content just to sniff.

Catnip experiences vary. Some fanciers have pleasurable encounters, like the one Silverbell G. describes: "The tingling starts in my tail and is followed by a full body rush that goes all the way to the tips of my whiskers." But some cats, like Lover Boy B., experience bad trips: "Say she throws me a new catnip mouse. During the first few minutes, the mouse and I are in love. I feel great! Then something happens. I flip out. If anyone comes near me, I'll scratch. I lose control and want to shred the mouse to bits."

And there can be too much of a good thing. With cats being downsized from their jobs, and vicious cat gangs on the rise, catnip abuse has grown, and nine-step recovery groups like CA have their paws full. In the hopes of steering impressionable kittens out of catnip fields and back to chasing butterflies, a "Just Meow No" campaign has been launched.

Trance Stances

Have you ever wondered why the cats pictured in ancient petroglyphs, Mayan pottery, Egyptian statues, and Native

American sand scratchings always look so spaced out? It's because they're all in a trance. Archeological investigation of these ritual cat postures has revealed that each unusual position produces its own unique, altered state.

For example, when assuming the posture of a tiny cat goddess discovered in a Maltese temple, sitting way back on her haunches with her right paw open and awkwardly raised, researchers all reported similar, and remarkable, sensations. They noted an increased heartbeat, stiff muscles, uncontrollable twitching in their whiskers and tail, and shivering. This was followed by a spirit journey to a world populated by animal guides.

Dr. Muffin Meed describes it well: "I fly up to the moon on the back of a crow. We float over the trees and suddenly a purple cloud in the sky opens and a great black jaguar leaps out, laps at my face, and takes my paw in his."

For the ordinary twentieth-century cat, Trance Stances let you position yourself in other realms and travel to other dimensions without leaving the kitchen. There's another plus. On interdimensional prowls, many cats report meeting spirit guides who become wonderful companions, advisers, and friends. "Spirit guides give so much and never try to grab your food or use your litter box," one enthusiastic tabby reports.

For the cat who's just starting to experiment with Trance

Stances, it's easier to keep your claws in both realities if you do the positions lying down.

High-Intensity Sound

In recent years, felines have become the victims of loud, industrial-age noise, and it's getting worse. Being able to hear sounds seven octaves above the human scale is no longer a blessing.

Research shows that resistance to loud sounds is what causes felines so much pain, and that acceptance is the answer. With this revelation, cats have begun to experiment by turning up the volume and tuning in. Cats have discovered that listening to high-intensity sound can actually transform acoustic pain into pleasure.

The technique is simple. You stretch out, close your eyes, relax, and become one with the sound, watching for the visions that come from deep within your psykitty. Then you turn both ears in the direction of the noise and welcome it with nonjudgmental acceptance.

You'll find that even the most irritating household sounds, like coffee grinders, vacuum cleaners, electric toothbrushes, boom boxes, and power mowers can transport you into altered states.

Holotropic Purrwork

A formidable Russian blue purrapsychologist named Stanislav Growl discovered that cats could achieve nonordinary states, and connect to "holos" or wholeness, by stretching out and purring rapidly without stopping, for hours on end. You might give it a try. One catveat: Purrwork can be very intense and may flip you forwards or backwards in time. If you have cold paws about reexperiencing in-utero life with your littermates, or a past life as a ferret, you'd better not do it alone.

The Whirling Dervish Technique

Here's a technique that will change your frequency. All you need is a cat "fishing rod" with a string and dangling lure on the end, and a person to whirl it around in circles. You chase after the lure. Soon you'll be spinning and whirling around wildly, totally disoriented, leaping and jumping, lost in the dance. The object is to keep your person playing until you spin out of consciousness and into an altered state.

This game is called the Whirling Dervish Technique after ancient Sufi cats, engaging in sacred all-night spinning frenzies, who found they could raise their vibrations and change their frequencies if they spun long enough.

SIX

Feline Future-Telling

Kitty Karma is when your past and present decide your future.
—Catmandu

What's our world coming to? As the clock ticktocks towards 2000, we're all clamoring for answers. Should you scoot out the catdoor and head for the Rockies, hang out with cat chat groups in cyberspace, join a feline survivalist community, crusade for animal and plant rights, or stay home and concentrate on raising your frequencies in order to ascend?

To answer these kinds of questions, many cats are rediscovering the ancient art of divination. Great mystics like Purrdmasambava tell us that the past, present, and future all exist simultaneously. You just need to know where to look.

Gazing into crystal balls, mouse holes, or paper bags isn't much different from reading entrails, consulting oracles, or unlocking the mysteries of your paw. It's not what you read, it's what you read into it. There's only one rule in future telling—patience.

Paw Reading

Warm paws, warm heart.
—Tabby affurism

In a Seattle coffeehouse, two cats curl up on a red velvet Victorian sofa in the back room. Madame Zolar, a mixed breed tabby with Gypsy blood, is about to do a reading on Mable, a black domestic shorthair with two fastidious white front paws. Mable asks what the future holds. Madame Zolar tells her to extend her right paw. Haltingly, Mable offers her immaculate small mitt, with claws curled in, concealing the pink pads on her paw. Madame Zolar sees this is going to be an easy reading. This cat's sensitive, spiritual, and afraid.

For thousands of years, felines have been fascinated by the secrets that are contained in the soft, furry folds of each pussy-cat's paw. Now that cats have more time on their paws and are delving into divination, paw reading is more popular than ever.

It seems that every nine lives you get a new set of possibilities and four new sets of paws. The front paws carry the possibilities, while the back ones help you carry them out. Whether you're destined to be a mystic or a mouser is inscribed in your tiny mitts from birth. Any cat can be a paw reader. To see what's in a paw, all you need is your All-Seeing Eye. A little purrapsychology also helps.

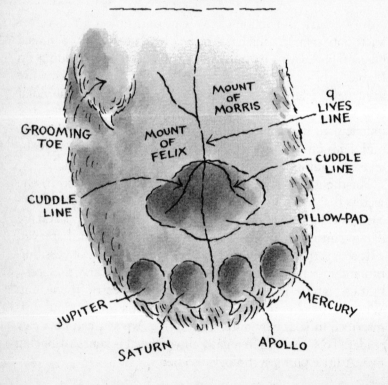

Unlike dogs, most cats don't offer their paws freely, and need to be coerced. Dabbing a little tuna on the reluctant querant's paw usually encourages them to open up. This is known as "crossing the paw with food," and began with Gypsy cat readers in ancient Egypt.

Traditionally, the right paw is read. Features such as paw size, shape, and length of mitt, along with pads, claws, fur texture, and fur tufts, further define the feline. Here are some basics.

PAW TYPES

Action Paws: Round paw. Tough, thick pads. Short, strong toes and claws. Scoops up food deftly. This paw type usually has a warm purrsonality, and makes friends easily. Good at self-defense. Morris is typical of this type.

Mental Paws: Oval paw. Delicate, chiseled-looking paw with long, dainty bones. Soft, round pads show extreme sensitivity. Well-groomed claws. Usually a high-strung intellectual type. Good linguists who enjoy conversing with humans. Frequently naps on the piano and PCs. Typical of Oriental shorthairs.

Technical Paws: Large, often massive paw. Rough pads. May have broken or missing claws. Dependable, resourceful creatures. Make good boxers. Excel at opening doors, drawers, turning on the TV, fishing without a rod. Typical of tomcats with territory of their own.

Emotional Paws: Big, soft, powder-puff paw. Well-developed, cushy pads are often pink and resemble pussy willows. This type of cat displays great delicacy and sensitivity, even in the hunt. Enjoys paw tickling from humans. Paws often emit high healing force when seen by cat sensitives. Typical of Persians, Birmans, Ragdolls.

Other Things to Examine

The Pillow-Pad. This is the foot's main cushion. An overly developed pillow-pad says the feline is a romantic dreamer, treads lightly over thorny issues, and has a penchant for soft spots. A pillow-pad that resembles a marshmallow suggests a cat who's lost touch with the earth and distances itself from reality. A pillow-pad that resembles shoe leather is found on a cat who's covered too many miles and could use a little rest.

The Grooming Toe. The fifth toe is a combination washcloth and loofah. It represents concerns about beauty and love. A well-developed toe suggests narcissism and may indicate a cat who is cut out for the cat show circuit.

Extra Toes. Having more than the standard-issue number of toes is the mark of a feline who's ready to take the next evolutionary steps.

Claws
- Extended claws show a belligerent nature.
- Retracted claws show a kind, trusting soul.
- Broken or missing claws can indicate a chronic nail-biter, athlete, or bully.
- Overly sharp claws indicate a cat who harbors deep hostility.
- Perfectly manicured claws show a cat who relates well to humans.

Boots
- Boots that go high up on the legs indicate modesty.
- Two matched boots show a well-balanced, fastidious animal who may object to sharing the litter box.
- A boot on the right paw shows the cat is eager to put its best foot forward.
- A boot on the left paw shows the cat is orderly and methodical in nature.

Fur
- Tufts of fur between the toes show an immature feline who enjoys being coddled like a baby.

- Different color fur between the toes suggests a colorful family background.
- Noticeably furry feet can be found on cats with secrets to hide.
- Long fur that makes walking difficult indicates aristocratic bloodlines.

The Mount of Felix: This pad is located at the top of the paw. When fat and full, it indicates a self-confident, independent, and good-natured feline. When flat, it suggests a fight-picking backbiter who lacks self-esteem.

The Mount of Morris: This pad represents an individual's charm, talent, and cuddliness. A pink, cushy pad shows an outgoing, gregarious nature, and someone who drops in for snacks at the neighbors. Underdeveloped pads are often found on couch shredders and finicky eaters.

Note: Watch how a cat uses its paws during a reading. Does it sit on them, lick them, groom them, stretch, or scratch at its fur? A cat who willingly offers its paw may indicate a recent past life as a dog. Good intuitive work only starts with the paws. The twitch of a tail, the angle of an ear, or the slightest movement of a whisker all convey distinct messages of their own.

Divination Techniques

Always finish a meal before you read the bones.
—Miss Cat Manners

From reading entrails to flipping twigs and consulting oracles, divination has been a time-honored way for felines to make a decision, or locate their next meal. Some ancient techniques, like this first one, are making a recent comeback, while others are new.

Reading Mouse Entrails

This ancient technique was first embraced by the early Roman cats who lived in and around the Colisseum, and is currently considered a politically correct divination technique because it recycles the mouse. All you do is ask a question and toss the mouse entrails up in the air with both paws. The way the bones fall provides the answer. For example:

Q. Will Purronious invite me to live in his nice, warm villa?
A. The leg bones have fallen in two X patterns. This means his villa is off-limits until you tidy up your mangy-looking coat.

Q. Where will I find my next meal?

A. Most of the bones have fallen to the east, which indicates that you should head in an easterly direction.

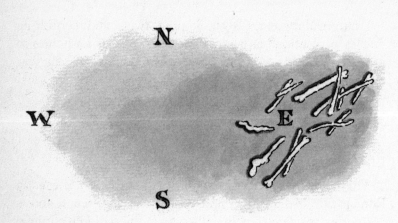

Kibble Reading

This contemporary divination technique allows you to do a reading while you eat. All it requires is a bowl of dry kibbles. What you do is:

1. Mark the directions around the bowl: North, South, East, and West.

2. Ask a question.

3. Knock the kibbles out of the bowl using one paw. Where the kibbles fall supplies your answer. For example:

> **Q.** Where can I meet the cat of my dreams?
> **A.** (Several kibbles have piled up in the North and the rest have landed in the South.) Leave through the north door of your house and walk due south. He or she will be waiting.

Note: Soft kibbles are unsuitable because they tend to clump.

Litter Box Readings

How centered are you today? Do your Kitty Chakras need to be balanced? You can get a quick read on your energy field every time you use the litter box. If it takes one simple paw maneuver to bury the evidence, you're well aligned. If it takes two or more scoops, go back to bed.

Heads or Tails?

Since most cats own one or more catnip mice, this technique is simple, and appeals to felines who don't like a lot of hocus-pocus. You decide whether the mouse's head or tail represents a "yes," ask your question, and flip the mouse up in the air. Feline psychics tell us that it's as reliable a method of future telling as any of the above.

The Oracle of Delfur

If you lack faith in your own divinations, the Oracle of Delfur is a reliable, if somewhat out of the way source. Since the days of Purracles and Socates, the Oracle has traditionally been a white angora who's never had a litter. As her powers are truly legendary, she's normally up to her whiskers in curious feline tourists who travel to Greece to see her.

The Oracle's tiny white temple sits right on the edge of the Mediterranean. She lies on a sun-bleached slab of white marble and interprets any strange movements or odd behavior in the fish who swim in the clear azure waters beneath her. The types and numbers of fish she spots, and what she finally catches between her paws, all help the Oracle form her answer. Sometimes she even shares her catch with the crowd.

SEVEN

Meows on the Millennium

Count your kittens, count your blessings, but
never ever count the years.
—Shakti Furball

Although it's recommended that you live in the Now and forget about the Then, the fascination with Millennium prophesies is reaching a feverish pitch. For most cats the underlying question is: Will the timing of my meals or the quality of food on my plate be disturbed by any possible planetary change?

Along with purrdictions from Nostracatus, Bastet, and invisible entities from the Purrides, cats are giving channeled maps of the future and stories about feline-noids from outer space as much attention as they would a spider building its web.

If you believe in Reincatnation, as most felines do, then even the gloomiest doomsday prophesies aren't cause for alarm. You know that after nine lives there are a myriad more, and life and death are just two sides of the catdoor. A mouser

who came over on the *Mayflower* may come back to be the
first feline on a trip to Mars.

To have the upper paw in your future, just don't imagine a
reality you don't like. To think it is to create it. Use the warm
space between your ears to conjure up images of interspecies
harmony on a contented Cat Mother Earth. Positive thoughts,
combined with heartfelt purrs, act as powerful, radiant prayers.
A little feline philosophy can also help. By asking "to what
purrpose?" each time life hands you a new snarled tangle of
mats, it's possible to enjoy sound catnaps even when those
around you appear to be aimless balls of flying fur.

The Purrdictions of Nostracatus and Others

Some purrdictions are like fleas.
They make you uncomfortable.
—Manx maxim

Perhaps the most famous of all feline prophets is Nostracatus. Although this brilliant French tabby saw his visions way
back in the 1500s, his meows about the future have been so
astonishingly accurate that his purrdictions are still being
investigated and decoded today.

Nostracatus was no average tabby tom. Before he was a prophet, he was one of the greatest healers of the sixteenth century, traveling from barn to barn and hamlet to hamlet, laying on paws and ministering to needy felines along the way. It was during one free moment of mousing that Nostracatus became connected to his greatest gift. Gazing into the empty blackness of a mouse hole, he saw more than the possibility of a forthcoming meal. This portal provided him with a magical "looking in" device that proved to be a doorway into the future, as the mouse hole "screen" began to show him incredible images of things to come.

To escape from persecution, since feline prophesy was forbidden, Nostracatus disguised his predictions by working them into elaborate paw print designs called "Pawtrains." Over the centuries devoted scholars have been able to coax out the elaborate prophetic messages that are hidden within.

The Purrdictions of Nostracatus

– The coming of the Three Anticats (cat haters):
  Napoleon (ailurophobe)
  Tweety Bird (chased to distraction by Sylvester)
  Fido Abdul (a canine born in the Middle East in 1985)

— The demise of cats who consorted with witches during the Dark Ages.
— The demand for cats who consort with witches in the late twentieth century.
— The coming of an animal rights movement.
— War breaking out between two territorial toms in Eastern Europe.
— The appearance of cats on "screens of theater."
— A land mass rising out of the Caribbean that reveals itself to be the lost continent of Catlantis.
— The emergence of feline weather oracles who predict earthquakes.
— A new strain of fleas who prove to be allergic to cats.
— The invention of an electromagnetic detangling wand.
— The discovery of a planet covered in cat litter that's hospitable to feline life.
— The discovery that sustained purring extends nine lives significantly.
— The advent of an era when humans study feline languages in school.
— Feline air travel in the baggage section.

The Visitations of Bastet

One current source of Millennium prophesies is the modern visitations of the ancient Egyptian Cat Goddess, Bastet. Bastet's first reappearance occurred back in 1917, when she began meowing messages about the future of the world to three frolicking kittens on Santa Catalina Island off the California coast.

As news of the Miracle of Santa Catalina spread, crowds of reverent cats blanketed the island, hoping to hear a prediction or see the kittens' tiny ecstatic whiskered faces peering up at the Cat Goddess. When a vacationing family from Chicago decided to adopt the kittens and take them home to the Midwest, the visions of Bastet came to an end.

More recently, Bastet has reappeared in Egypt. When a feline resident of the Cairo Museum reported that one of the Bastet statues had begun to leak milk from her paws, thousands of seekers flocked to the site while an Egyptian dairy company dispensed free saucers of milk. At the ruins of Beni Hassan, three thousand cats gathered, hoping to see a well-publicized angry and hissing appurrition of Bastet that a family of Egyptian Maus claimed to have seen. This unearthly hissing was found to be a hoax.

At Rome's Colisseum, an all-night vigil attracted fifteen thousand felines who gathered to see a sign from the Cat Goddess. Some say they saw a giant can of tuna, while others describe a ten-story mouse.

The Purrdictions of Bastet

- The shift from a dog-fixated society to a cat-fixated society.
- Wet litter boxes as a result of global flooding.
- Strange weather patterns that cause your fur to grow one minute and shed the next.
- The arrival of barking canine-noids from Sirius, the Dog Star.
- The disappearance of the Apple Head Siamese.
- The appearance of a hairless Sphinx.
- A shift of the earth's axis, resulting in two suns, and mass confusion about when it's time to eat.
- The discovery of a road map of the future chiseled into the Sphinx's right paw.
- In 1999, the Year of the Cat in Chinese astrology, a female Abyssinian from Ohio will be recognized as the reincarnation of the first Dalai Lama's favorite gray tabby.
- The Second Coming of Felix the cat in 2002.
- The unearthing of ancient artifacts, which predate Cat-lantis and Lemewria, from an advanced civilization of giant cats.
- A blue healing ray that produces an odd blue glow around your fur.

- A change in your feline frequency, which causes you to suddenly lose your footing or have your tail fur bristle at the slightest sound.
- A period of "Great Cleansing" when cats all over the planet begin to give themselves more baths.
- Conclusive proof that the cats of ancient Egypt came from Orion.
- The discovery of parallel dimensions where you don't need to use a litter box.

Catsey, the Catnapping Prophet

One of the most famous feline prophets began as a hard-working mouser on a Shenendoah Valley farm. One day, back in the 1920s, a blinding, white light stopped him in the middle of a hunt. "What would you like to do with your life besides catching mice?" a voice asked. Without even one indecisive flip of his tail, Catsey quickly answered: "Help my fellow felines."

Catsey was given a great gift. He became the Catnapping Prophet, receiving his visions while he snoozed on a favorite tattered sofa. Twitching whiskers signaled his calico wife, who asked questions and scratched notes while he snoozed.

Catsey would travel in his astral furbody and prescribe remedies for cats who were often very far away. Although his purrdictions were amazingly accurate, he never remembered a second of them, and would always wake up, wash his whiskers, stretch, and head for supper on the kitchen floor. In spite of his enormous notoriety, Catsey remained a modest feline who liked to remind us: "I'm a mouser, not a saint."

Catsey's Purrdictions

- The advent of canned cat food.
- A 1929 panic where working felines lose their jobs.
- A cat on the moon, although possibly in its astral body.
- The emergence of cats as America's most popular pet.
- Humans disguised as felines, singing and dancing on a stage.
- The collapse of color and point barriers between Siamese breeds.
- The disappearance of the pedigree as the benchmark of superior feline breeding.
- A cure for fur balls composed of blue-green algae and Dalmatian dander.
- The discovery of the Dead Sea Scratchings.
- A cat in the White House by 1992.
- The invention of rip-proof fibers that bring long talons back into vogue.

Cat Channelers

*There are as many cat spirits involved in cat life at this
moment as there are cats.*
—Rampurr

"I was ready to hear about the real meaning of life," says Tootsie
V., a tortie tabby mother of four litters from San Jose, California.
"After mousing, mating, raising kittens, and repeated investiga-
tions of both the basement and the attic, I knew there was more."

Tootsie ended up at the paws of a trance channeler, who,
she purrs, changed her life. "My channeler is in touch with
several entities, but the one who had a profound effect on me
was the Persian cat of a carpet dealer from Afghanistan. He
knew everything about me, even when I hid in the neighbor's
garage for three days, and he showed me that I'm completely
responsible and can change my life."

Tootsie V. is typical of a growing segment of the feline
population who are seeking spiritual guidance from chan-
nelers. These days, many of the startling revelations about the
Millennium are coming through ordinary felines who act as
"fur vehicles" for disembodied entities, guides, and helpers
from the other side. Entities like Rampurr, Emmanuel Fluff-
ball, and spirits from the Purrides constellation often meow
through ordinary house cats and sound like affected Siamese.

Rampurr, who claims to be the spirit of a thirty-thousand-year-old saber-toothed tiger, speaks through a mild-mannered orange tabby named Marmalade. The evening that Rampurr chose to make his first appearance, Marmalade was batting crystals around the kitchen floor. Suddenly, her whiskers began to vibrate, her ears twitched, and she fell into a swoon. As she drifted into a catnap/trance, the spirit of Rampurr crawled in.

Rampurr claims that his mission is to help cats regain their self-esteem. "You have lost touch with your wild, instinctive nature and need to use your claws again. There will be upon this plane a coming which is called 'The Reality with More Teeth,'" he says. Rampurr, who growls and hisses as he delivers his messages, has been nicknamed "The Snarling Sage."

Though she remembers nothing of Rampurr's visits, Marmalade says they leave her feeling like she's "enjoyed a good stretch."

Map of the Future

Never get too comfortable on the bed.
—Swami Purrananda

According to one feline source, earth changes are about to alter Cat Mother Earth's outer appearance more dramatically than a Persian with a lion cut.

While catnapping, Bootsie Adair, a calico mother of six litters from Minneapolis, Minnesota, was shown a map of the future by a group of Ascended Cat Masters that included Bastet, Kwan Yin Yowl, Saint Morris, Kathumi, Felix the Protector, Sylvestor the Watchful, and Swami Purrananda. Their message: The time of the "Great Cleansing" is at paw and Cat Mother Earth is about to sit up, stretch, shake out her dusty fur coat, work out the nasty mats, and give herself a thorough bath that will result in the rearrangement of the existing landmasses and their surrounding seas.

Bootsie Adair knew this message from the Ascended Cat Masters was of great importance, and maps of the future Catworld can now be found in homes everywhere.

However, the Ascended Cat Masters suggest that cats can avert this "Great Cleansing" by cleaning up Cat Mother Earth themselves while she sleeps. They say "a Big Licking" could put things back into balance and make her fur coat, now adversely affected by the ravages of pollution and poor grooming, regain its former luster and shine.

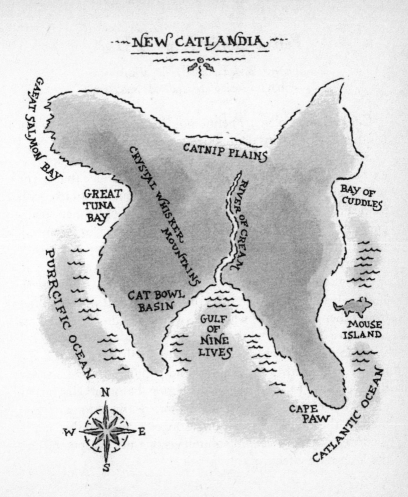

Feline-noids Among Us?

They've landed and they have whiskers!
—From *Invasion of the Cat Body Snatchers*

Cats on other planets? Feline-noid visitors right here on Cat Mother Earth? Aliens disguised as tabby neighbors? Why not?

Since the early 1950s, reports of all kinds of strange, extraterrestrial phenomena have led cats to believe that in the universal scheme of things, they're not alone. Contacts with feline entities from other planets, abductions onto alien space-craft, and trips to alien planets have all been experienced, investigated, and well documented.

Many cats sense that feline-noids from other planets and solar systems are presently living among us, along with "Crawl-ins," who are described as disembodied purrsonalities from other dimensions who take over the bodies of adult cats who have decided to move on.

Some of these whiskered extraterrestrials may even come from planets with totally feline-noid populations. Experts say they've come to warn our own cat population about current planetary conditions that could prove hazardous. These include the continued consumption of overly mushy, mass-produced cat food, sleeping on televisions and computers, and the long-term effects of catnip.

Just where do these alien cat entities, feline-noids, and "crawl-ins" come from? The Purrides constellation, Vega, Lyra, Arcaturus, Catsiopeia, and Zeta Recatulum are most frequently mentioned. Some of the aliens, like those from the Purrides, have friendly reputations, while rumor has it that others aren't so nice.

The Grays

An often spotted (though seldom striped or dotted) group among these feline-noid visitors are known as the "Grays," and are described as gray shorthairs with sparse fur, meager whiskers, huge slanted pitch black eyes, and a virtually nonexistent nose and mouth. The buzz is that some of them come from Orion, and some from Zeta Recatulum.

What's brought them here? Apparently, they are impressed by all the varieties of Seafood Supper on this planet and have grown weary of the candidates for courtship back home.

Many felines believe that humans are wise to the Grays and their intentions, and have been conducting a massive cover-up operation since the Grays crashed in New Mexico in the 1940s. They say that humans captured a Gray and his cat dish and discovered that it was made from a strange substance not found on earth.

Some even go on to say that this captured Gray was eventually interbred with a hairless sphinx, and that their odd looking descendants can be spotted in cat shows today. There's further speculation that humans are allowing the Grays to woo beautiful feline Earthlings, feeding them all the Sheba and Fancy Feast they want in exchange for advanced kitty litter technology.

Was Morris Abducted?

All this talk of alien intervention and abduction makes a cat wonder: Is Honeybun really Honeybun or some feline-noid from outer space? And what actually became of Morris? Did he pass on, or was he, as some say, abducted from his dressing room by "visitors" from outer space? Hopefully, time will provide answers to all these questions, and more.

Catnip Crop Circles

Meanwhile Millennium madness spreads, along with new accounts of strange and unexplainable phenomena. One of the most fascinating is Catnip Crop Circles. These huge, intricate geometric designs, which are so gigantic they can be

surveyed only by climbing to the tops of trees, resemble large feline masks, or cat bodies, complete with paws and tails.

The patterns are always etched into catnip fields that are ready to be harvested, and the catnip plants are bent but never broken. Investigators have also discovered that the cell structure of the catnip plants have been mysteriously altered and any cat who rolls around in a Catnip Crop Circle, or chews on a plant, experiences unpleasant buzzing sensations and starts meowing in strange tongues.

What's causing the Catnip Crop Circles? Some invisible, mysterious force. These "cat agriglyphs," as they're called, are always formed at night, and not one of the many hundreds of cats who patiently sit in the catnip fields waiting for something to happen has ever seen how.

How Odd

Other random, yet possibly related reports include the disappearance of hundreds of Bumble Bee tuna trucks all over the country, microscopic implants found on the ears of cat abductees, stories of iridescent gray fur showing up on furniture and clothes, and the circulation of an underground tape called "Meows from the Purrides," which is said to be channeled greetings from another star system.

Recent Surveys

For the older cat population, all this feline-noid talk is disturbing. Anything that might mean competition at the food dish or rivalry for space on the sofa is best avoided. But most kittens express an interest in visiting other star systems and say they'd welcome visitors, with or without tails. Recent surveys show that 70 percent of the feline population accept the possibility of a higher form of feline intelligence existing on another planet. Thirty percent believe they may be smart, but they couldn't be that smart if they still need spaceships to get here. And over 80 percent of the world's Siamese cat population categorically refuse to believe there's feline intelligence anywhere in the universe that's smarter than them.

EIGHT

Insights and Inspurration

Climb on the roof and sing your note.
—Rumeeow

Even the most clear-sighted feline navigators of the night are groping for new directions. Cats are flocking to bookstores, lying on the New Age stacks for inspurration, and soaking up the meowings of mystical poets and the insights of feline visionaries through their fur.

Many felines say the return of the Cat Goddess is also of great significance. As we awaken from "The Great Catnap" and prepare for "The Great Cleansing," we look for new answers, preparing ourselves for the long stretch of more harmonious and enlightened living that's expected to come.

The Mystical Poetry of Rumeeow

For inspiration, millions of twentieth-century felines are listening to meows from the distant past: the great thirteenth-century poet and prophet, Rumeeow.

This whirling silver-blue Persian Sufi, who expressed his intoxication for the sacred being who dwells within each of us, wrote over thirty thousand mystical poems. Rumeeow's work connects us to the glory of creation that's reflected all around us, and reminds us to be passionate and purrful in our adoration of what we're given each day.

Why are you chasing shadows all the time?
What do you wish to wash from your fur with your paws?
You are sacred from head to feet to tail.
Oh, naive cat, what are you looking for
Beyond yourself?

*

When I am with you, we prowl and purr together all night.
When you're not here, I can't even catnap.
Praise the Heavens for these two insomnias!
And the difference between them.

*

Today, like every other day,
we wake up empty and anxious.
Don't climb on your human's bed and begin meowing.
Jump on the windowsill and purr in the fresh morning air.

*

Let the beauty be celebrated.
There are hundreds of ways to kiss the earth by rolling on the
ground.

*

Out beyond ideas of scratching or not scratching the Oriental
carpets, there is a field.
I'll meet you there.
When the soul lies down in that grass,
the world is too full to meow about.

Even the notion of giving each other a bath doesn't make any
sense.

*

Don't treat me like a stray.
I am your neighbor.
My house is close to yours.
I may look mangy, but my heart is good.
My inside is shining even if my meowings are obscure.

*

All of our nine lives we've looked into each other's faces.
That was the case today too.

How do we keep our love a secret?
We speak from whiskers to whiskers
and hear with our eyes and our tails.

*

I used to hide under the camel.
You made me sing.

I used to walk away from the platter.
Now I cry for plates of fresh poultry.

In somber dignity, I used to lie
in the sun and contemplate the tip of my tail.

Now kittens run across my back
and chew on my ears.

Return of the Cat Goddess:
The End of a Dog-Eat-Dog Society

The wind is Cat Mother Earth's purr.
—Calico cat saying

One of the most pivotal transformations now taking place on the planet has to do with the species in power. There's a sociopolitical movement underfoot and the feet belong to cats instead of dogs. We're all ready to be unleashed as the Divine Feline makes her return.

This shift from dog to cat power spells the end of dogriarchal society (dog worshiping) and the beginning of a catriarchal society (cat worshiping). It's a change that's destined to affect the attitudes we have about everything, from how we treat Cat Mother Earth to the values we'll ascribe to things like sleep, serenity, self-reliance, and cleanliness for millennia to come.

The Waning of Dog Days

For over two thousand years the ancient Egyptians worshiped the Cat Goddess, Bastet, but for centuries now, the cat has been the underdog.

We've seen a world dominated by canine values and dog-based beliefs. In Fido culture, rolling over, shaking paws, loyalty, and perfect obedience have garnered rewards. This has resulted in a society of pit bulls who will do anything for gain and approval-hungry canines hanging on by their teeth. But times are changing. Now that cats have landed jobs in the White House and surpassed dogs in pet popularity contests, all those somersaulting poodles, brandy-toting Saint Bernards, and newspaper-fetching golden retrievers are beginning to wonder if they've been handed the wrong end of the rawhide bone.

A Softer, More Sensual Time

Look forward to an age of renewed sensuality. From the joys of licking and cleaning your own fur to the pleasures of grooming others, a new body-consciousness will appear. The cries of unabashed sensuality will be heard on every corner as once again cats hold their tails high and all creatures rediscover their natural sexuality as a source of delight.

The Divine Cat Mother will bring tender mothering to needy kittens everywhere, restoring harmony and balance. It will be a time of initiation into all that is mysterious, fertile, beautiful, natural, intuitive, and sensate, as we rediscover the

Divine Feline who lives within each one of us. Bastet is returning to a world desperately in need of feline values.

New Dogma of the Cat

The old doggerel is on its way out. Our catriarchal society will flourish from its feline-based beliefs. Here are some examples.

Serenity is the measure of success.
You can tell a lot about a cat by the quality of its purr.
Eat when you want.
Go where you wish.
Always make room for a friend.
You are a kitten of Cat Mother Earth. Treat her with respect.
Trees are not fire hydrants. They are there to be climbed.
There's no such thing as too much sleep.
Investigate all food before putting it in your mouth.
Don't do anything to please people unless it pleases you.
Be as sensual as you feel.
You can never be too clean.
Always smell like yourself.
Don't perform for anyone.
Sniff everything first.

Encourage your kittens to become cats.
Leave the forest the way you found it.
Be graceful in all you do.
Live happily with little.
Worship everything that moves.
Make a goddess of the moon.
Let the sun be your God.

NINE

Millennium Astrology Forecast

Celestial bodies above, fur bodies below.
—Catpurrnicus

Most cats already know their astrological sign. To find out how the Millennium may be affecting you, we've consulted some of felinedom's top astrologers to bring you these Tails of the Zodiac.

Aries

March 21–April 19

Threats to de-legalize catnip? A new ban on wind-up mice? A feline uprising against the soaring cost of kitty litter? You'll lead the charge! Forever ready to defend your territory, as well as Cat Mother Earth's, feisty Mars-ruled Aries cats will rush headlong into whatever's new and exciting in the next century without sniffing first.

ARIES

Be on the Prowl For: As planetary action speeds up, it may go to your head and make you dizzy. You'll bump into furniture and may develop a slight ringing in your already wartorn ears.

A Meow to the Wise: Don't bare your claws at every new cause or you'll exhaust your reserves. Choose your battles wisely and find someone to scratch you around your ears, face, and neck.

Taurus

April 20–May 20

Blue-green algae catfood in a capsule? No way! As a Venus-ruled earth-kitty and fur-bearing bull, grazing on real food, digging in the dirt, and rolling in the grass are pleasures you don't want progress to take away. If you're forced to make do with Feline Virtual Reality, get used to stalking virtual birds and virtual grasshoppers and sniffing virtual flowers in the virtual woodlands of your choice.

TAURUS

Be on the Prowl For: Your Taurean materialism could make you prey to counterfeit Rolex cat collars, forged celebrity pawgraphs, or Moon cat litter scams.

A Meow to the Wise: For security, stockpile catnip toys. In times of stress put your paws over your ears and purr yourself to sleep.

Gemini

May 21–June 20

Fun-loving Gemini cat—maybe you should reconsider that Millennium party you're planning to throw at the Pet Super Store! The morning after all those bone-slinging canines and catnip-infused kitties have frolicked in the aisles won't be a pretty sight! It's time to start using your clever Mercurial mind for interspecies communication. Try making better contact with humans first.

Be on the Prowl For: Your love of travel could steer you far afield. As unseen worlds collide you might end up in a strange backyard on Andromeda or chasing astral butterflies on the astral plane.

GEMINI

A Meow to the Wise: If you and your twin end up on different frequencies, give your aura a good cleaning, and follow it with an amethyst rub-up to wind down.

Cancer

June 21–July 22

All this yowling about earth changes will propel you Cancer kitties to burrow deeper under the old heirloom quilt, dragging some of your favorite kitty keepsakes along for company. But hiding like a Crab can't go on for too long. As the cat mother of the zodiac, you'll want to teach your New Age kittens old-fashioned cat family values, and make sure they still have a beautiful planet to play on and plenty of cream.

CANCER

Be on the Prowl For: To avoid wet paws, get up-to-the-minute flood warnings by psychically hooking up to your ruler, the Moon. In times of lunacy, steer clear of sleazy salescats trying to peddle rubber-lined Kitty Kozies that float.

A Meow to the Wise: Although your tendency is to dig your claws into everything you love and not let go, learn to detach, without being crabby.

Leo

July 23–August 22

Theatrical Leo pussycats, time to create a reality in which you're the star! Why limit your glamour puss to all those shaky home videos that make your golden eyes look red when you could be The Feline Face of 2000, appearing on billboards, TV and computer screens, and in holograms beamed to other universes! You might even sell a line of jeweled cat accessories on your own home shopping network!

LEO

Be on the Prowl For: Watch the way you shake your mane! Alien toms may want to mix with you. Try not to let gentle neck bites and flattering meows make you mother of a new breed without your consent.

A Meow to the Wise: For spiritual growth, learn to do without weekly comb-outs at the grooming parlor and a purrsonal trainer to take you through your morning stretches.

VIRGO

Virgo

August 23–September 22

Most meticulous Virgo kitties have already begun the New Age task of cleaning up their lives. Your neatly scratched self-improvement list includes: daily purification baths to keep your aura pristine, yoga catsanas, no canned catfood (not enough life force), donating all but one toy (a well-chewed catnip vet doll) to needy strays, and volunteer purr therapy with the elderly. A roll in the mud will do you some good.

Be on the Prowl For: Use your keen Mercurial powers of discrimination to sniff out sleeping spots with good Kitty Chi, flea-free paths to enlightenment, and leaders who are passionate about animal rights.

A Meow to the Wise: Why lose fur worrying over what happens next? No matter what cat clairvoyants purrdict, the future is never what you expect.

Libra

September 23–October 22

In the coming era, expect beautiful Venus-ruled Libra love-cats to crusade for fairer and more meaningful relationships. If someone grabs you by the scruff of the neck and meows "let's make kittens," you'll answer with a hiss. Even humans will need reminding. Once-a-week brushings, the occasional snuggle, or a quick scratch under the chin are poor substitutes for real love.

LIBRA

Be on the Prowl For: The catnip's always greener on the other side of the galaxy. Overly solicitous suitors, masquerading as suave British shorthairs, may try luring you off the planet with meows about cream and crabmeat crumpets from the Milky Way.

A Meow to the Wise: If the increased magnetic pull of the moon turns your magnificently coifed fur coat into a static mess, learn to live with it. Bad fur days don't mean the end of the world.

Scorpio

October 23–November 21

For Pluto-ruled pussycats who enjoy spooky stuff, your time is at paw. Expect to see appurritions, channel cats from the Purrides, read human minds, levitate the birds off the trees, and become irresistible to the dog. Your animal magnetism will be at a feverish pitch, and whiskered friends will be lining up at the catdoor for readings. Hang up your Paw Reader/Adviser sign and get to work.

Be on the Prowl For: You've always suspected that the neighbor's Siamese isn't really a Siamese. He rarely meows and has a peculiar, alien smell. Use your Scorpio detective skills to investigate.

A Meow to the Wise: Watch what you meow. A misplaced hiss could lead to unpleasant cat spats. With more intense energy, friends will be more sensitive than usual.

SCORPIO

Sagittarius

November 22–December 20

Travel-loving Sagittarian pussycats can really take off in the Aquarian Age. Antigravity Kitty Kozies, jet-packed litter boxes, and holographic visualization techniques will carry you farther than your family's summer cabin in Maine. But watch your wanderlust! Too many out-of-furbody adventures can mean missed meals and worried humans back home. Come the Millennium, staying grounded will be your greatest challenge.

Be on the Prowl For: Look for new cat religions. Representatives from the Mystic Cats Coven, Holy Roaming Catlicks, Catafarians, Hare Katmas, Holy Rollovers, Templars of Bastet, Purrly Gaters, and Nine-Lives Adventists may all be dropping leaflets by your catdoor.

A Meow to the Wise: If cats meowing doomsday messages make your fur stand on end, turn on your sunny disposition and purr bright light into their energy fields.

SAGITTARIUS

CAPRICORN

Capricorn

December 21–January 19

Come the Millennium, Capricorn kitties may be considering politics, or similar leadership roles. Perched on the roof like a mountain goat, you're sad to see that feline standards have plummeted to the basement, where hardworking mousers used to be! And if elected to the First Feline World Forum, you'll bring back traditional values like fishing, hunting, and foraging for a living, and teaching the kittens to do more than play with yarn and watch TV.

Be on the Prowl For: As an enterprising Saturn-ruled pussycat, New Age items like aura brushes and combs, Bach Flower Flea Remedies, and herbal scratching posts could spell big business opportunities for you.

A Meow to the Wise: When your whiskers start drooping from dark, dour thoughts, climb up a tree, abandon all Capricorn reserve, and just howl.

Aquarius

January 20–February 18

Uranus-ruled pussycat, with your hot pink claws and whiskers dipped in sparkles, you are the future and this is your age! If you decide to hang tiny magnets from your tail to see if

AQUARIUS

they attract members of the opposite sex, join a kitty commune or organize giant global Purr-Ins—nobody will bat a whisker. Somebody's got to lead the Feline Revolution to Awaken Planetary Cat Consciousness. It may as well be you!

Be on the Prowl For: Astral cat entities may try to borrow your body. To avoid becoming a "crawl in," make sure your silver cord stays connected to your sleeping body when you're on the astral prowl.

A Meow to the Wise: Sparking, crackling fur with an odd, blue glow around it is the price you may have to pay for a higher frequency. To encourage petting, and to avoid a frightful furstyle, roll in Omega 3 fish oil twice a day.

Pisces

February 19–March 20

As the escape artist of the zodiac, you dreamy fur fish are always looking for ways to slip out of bed and into other dimensions. During the coming age, visiting a past life in Catlantis, a future life on your ruling planet, Neptune, or astral projecting yourself into the aquarium will be commonplace.

By using your mind, you'll also run and walk less, which means no more aching Pisces paws!

Be on the Prowl For: When it comes to deciding how to celebrate the Millennium, you could be chasing your tail in different directions. There's the Harmonious Convergence of Cats being held at the Sphinx, and the all-you-can-eat gala at Sheba headquarters. Better flip a chicken bone for the answer.

A Meow to the Wise: Planetary changes will result in a new strain of catnip seventy times more potent than normal. If you're prone to catnip abuse, it's best to steer clear.

PISCES

TREATS

Always be on the prowl for the Truth.
—Thich Ncat Tomk

Workshops

Our editors have chosen several select workshops from the many that are currently being offered all over the world.

Tomcat Weekend Warrior Training

For neutered male toms who've been overly pampered and protected, the Weekend Warrior Training is a chance to reclaim your identity as you bond with other boy cats. Namby-pamby house kitties will benefit from this chance to trade the soft life for a rough 'n tumble weekend in the Catscade mountain wilderness. Stalk, sniff, scratch, mark your territory. Climb

trees. Scramble through the underbrush. Hunt and eat your own prey. Fully stocked woodland dining experience. The workshop promises you'll go home a new tom. Write: Blackie Blye's Tomcat Weekend Warriors, Rt. 999, Deep Woods, Maine.

Yowling: Finding Your Own Voice, Finding Your Own Song

What stops you from caterwauling at the top of your lungs? Self-criticism? Fear of upsetting the humans who feed you? Or fear of having a water pistol fired at your fur? Whatever it is, this workshop will help you break the silence and reclaim your unique feline voice. Taught by Guido Purrvarotti, the famous Italian tabby troubadour, in soundproof studios, you'll learn how to evoke your own personal mews, and find expressive new ways with a shriek, screech, yowl, caterwaul, snarl, or hiss. Write: Yowling Workshop, Omega Institute for Felines, Rhinebark, New York.

"Katra Sutra": A Workshop in Feline Sexuality

If you're a tom who wants his pick of the Queens, or a Queen who'd like to reign in more toms, this workshop is for

you. According to feline sex expert Ravi Katma, there's more to sex than you learned in the woods. Ravi is a dashing eastern Ocicat renowned for his liberal interpretation of the Katra Sutra, an eight-thousand-year-old Indian manual on feline sexuality, and for his exciting, "paws-on" material. In this weeklong workshop, you and multiple partners will explore new kinds of furplay and mating techniques. Write: Ravi Katma, Purradise Island, The Bahamas.

Coven of Cats: Witchcraft Rediscovery Weekend

This weekend offers a chance to recapture those pagan energies and put some magic back in your life. Resident Warlock Aleister Growley leads the cat coven in ritual magic exercises, with special emphasis on spells for cats seeking new mates. There's also a night of Wiccat in the woods. Write: Witchcraft Rediscovery Weekend, Blackmass Lane, Salem, Massachusetts.

Feline Firewalking

Although more than fifty thousand cats have walked on fire since 1982, this hot Hawaiian workshop, billed as a tool for

feline purification and transformation, is not recommended for cats who like to pussyfoot around. You'll enjoy warm-up strolls across hot lava, followed by brisk walks across twenty-foot beds of smoking charcoal. Firewalk leader Tawny Roberts, a fiery brown shorthair, teaches you confidence-building mantras to meow before you take the big hike. Write: Feline Firewalks, Hot Pau Pau Island, Hawaii.

Purrananda Ashram Getaways

Felines looking for a weekend of enlightenment might consider the Purrananda Ashram in the Catskills, where the svelte and beautiful Bombay, Guru Meow, is top cat. Disciples of the Guru purr about her power to awaken your Kitty Kundalini with her "Shakti-Pet." The daily schedule includes Catsang, yoga catsanas, chanting, teachings from the Guru, blessings from the Guru, and glossy coat tips from the Guru. It also includes time spent in selfless service, such as cleaning litter boxes or picking cat fur off the ashram's many soft cushions. Write: Purrananda Ashram, South Fleasberg, New York.

A Millennium Meditation

Great Whiskered Ones! Ascended Cat Masters! Bastet! Morris! Rumeeow! Feline Spirit Guides! Great White Angora Brotherhood! Lords of Kitty Karma! Angelcats everywhere! I humbly kneel on all-fours asking for your collective help and divine guidance:

I now call forth an all-powerful beam of Cosmic Light to surround and shield me from this moment on into the next Millennium.

I see this Cosmic Light bathing my entire being.

I now call forth the full opening of My All-Seeing Eye and all my psychic abilities, so that I may use them to the benefit of all creatures.

I now call forth the complete activation of my Kitty Kundalini.

I now call forth the complete balancing of my Kitty Karma from all my past and future lives.

I now call forth the perfect attunement I need to fulfill my earthly mission in this span of nine lives.

I now call forth a full awakening into Higher Kitty Consciousness.

I vow that from this day forward, onward into the next Millennium, no matter what life puts on my plate, I will always find reasons to purr.

I pray that light and love bring Cat Mother Earth and all her kittens into a time of great peace and harmony.

GLOSSARY OF TERMS

Mean what you mean.
—The Random Mouse Dictionary

Affurmation: A statement that affurms what is.
Ascended Cat Masters: Feline spiritual advisers on the astral plane.
Astral plane: The unseen world.
Astral furbody: Your spirit body.
Aromatherapy: Using scent as a healing tool.
Aura: The egg-shaped envelope of electromagnetic activity that surrounds you.
Aura fluffing: Rearranging the energy so your aura is in top cat-show condition.
Cat Enneagram: A map of feline behavior and motivation that includes nine purrsonality types.
Catnip Crop Circles: Unexplained large, intricate geometric patterns discovered in catnip fields.

Catriarchal: Feline values.

Catropratic: A technique that realigns the spine with gentle manipulation.

Catsanas: Cat yoga postures.

Catsang: When feline spiritual seekers gather around their guru.

Catupressure: A technique where the paws poke deeply into the body in order to unlock the Kitty Chi.

Catzu: An ancient Oriental healing art that employs paw-poking techniques.

Chakra: A spinning vortex through which feline life force enters the furbody.

Channeling: Acting as a feline satellite dish for disembodied spirits.

Conscious Eating: A meditation technique in which you pay close attention to every aspect of your meal.

Crawl-in: When a cat from another dimension swaps places with a cat in this dimension by crawling into his or her body.

Dogriarchal: Canine values.

Eye of Morris: Egyptian symbol for the All-Seeing Eye.

Feline Archetypes: Typical reoccurring feline themes.

Feline-noid: An extraterrestrial cat.

Fur bodywork: Techniques that manipulate the furbody to restore health.

Higher Cat: The nonphysical, spiritual part of yourself.

Holotropic Purrwork: Sustained, deep purring in order to achieve nonordinary states.

Kitty Chi: The Oriental term for your feline life force, or purrana.

Kitty Karma: What you drag in from past lives.

Kitty Kundalini: The powerful transformational energy that lies curled up in a ball, like a sleeping kitten, at the base of your tail.

Kneading: Passing energy through your paws to a marching beat.

Laying on of paws: Healing techniques where the paws are used.

Mindful Purring: A meditation technique where you calm the mind by focusing on your purr.

Paw-scanning: Using your paws to feel where your aura is electrically matted or tangled.

Psykitty: Your inner cat.

Purrana: Feline life force.

Purranayama: Cat yoga breathing techniques.

Purrapsychology: A study of the inner mysteries of the pussycat psyche.

Purrides: The constellation of friendly feline-noids.

Purrsona: The outer mask you wear.

Rei-Kitty: A natural laying-on-of-paws healing technique from the Orient.

Reincatnation: A belief in life before and after nine lives.

Roughing: A form of therapeutic massage that releases blocks by roughing you up.

Shadow: The flip side of your purrsona that you deny, reject, or disown.

Shakti-Pet: A paw touch that has the power to awaken your Kitty Kundalini.

TM: A meditation technique that helps you Transcend constant thoughts about Meals.

Wiccat: Feline witchcraft.